The Small-Cap Investor

The Small-Cap Investor

Secrets to Winning Big with Small-Cap Stocks

IAN WYATT

WILEY

John Wiley & Sons, Inc.

Published by John Wiley & Sons, Inc., Hoboken, New Jersey.
Published simultaneously in Canada.

For general information on our other products and services or for technical support, please contact our Customer Care Department within the United States at (800) 762-2974, outside the United States at (317) 572-3993 or fax (317) 572-4002.

Wiley also publishes its books in a variety of electronic formats. Some content that appears in print may not be available in electronic books. For more information about Wiley products, visit our web site at www.wiley.com.

Library of Congress Cataloging-in-Publication Data:

Wyatt, Ian, 1980–
  The small-cap investor : secrets to winning big with small-cap stocks / Ian Wyatt.
     p. cm.
  Includes bibliographical references and index.
  ISBN 978-0-470-40526-0 (cloth)
  1. Small capitalization stocks.   2. Investments.   I. Title.
  HG4971.W93 2010
  332.63'22–dc22

                                                                  2009013306

Printed in the United States of America

10   9   8   7   6   5   4   3   2   1

To Gram and Grandpa Cheney
who got me started with investing

Contents

Acknowledgments

I want to thank the many people who contributed to this book in varying ways.

Thanks to my wonderfully supportive and loving wife, Carrie. Your constant feedback, critiques, and thorough editing have made this book something I am very proud of. Thank you for investing the time in this project, working with me during the evenings and weekends. And thank you for your endless support in my professional and personal life.

Thanks to my loving parents, Bruce and Carol, for supporting my interest in the stock market from an early age, helping me find great learning experiences, and encouraging me to start my own business, taking the path less taken.

Thanks to my sister, Jocelyn, and brother, Reid, for loaning me money to invest in the stock market, my first childhood experience with leverage.

Thanks to my collaborator on this project, Michael Thomsett. I enjoyed working with you to put together a great book—hopefully the first of many.

I also want to thank all of my colleagues at Business Financial Publishing who contributed to this project. To my editor, Bob Bogda, I've learned much from you over the years. To my talented researchers, Benson George and Jason Cimpl, thank you for setting aside your regular jobs to help find the examples that made this book what it is. And thank you to everyone else at my company who allowed me the time to write this book.

IAN WYATT

The Small-Cap Investor

INTRODUCTION

The Story of a Small-Cap Investor

There is nothing quite as exciting, intoxicating, or rewarding as investing in promising *small-cap* stocks—those on the path to growth, profits, and big returns for their shareholders. I love investing in small-cap stocks, those publicly traded companies with market capitalizations of less than $2 billion. My favorite and best-performing investments of all time have tended to be the smallest of the small caps, with market capitalization of less than $500 million; these are often called *micro* caps. I like to discover the unknown stock with great promise and strong fundamentals when nobody else has recognized the potential. And I try to buy growth at value prices.

Many great small-cap stocks go unnoticed by other investors, not only by individuals, but by big institutional investors as well. This book tells you why these stocks are usually overlooked, and shows you how to find the small companies with significant potential for growth and profits. It also shows you how to evaluate these stocks from both a fundamental and a technical perspective so you can determine whether you should buy the stock to begin with, and also when you should buy and sell. Small caps are different than mid- or large-cap stocks in many ways, and can yield significant gains that are impossible to find in larger stocks. Unfortunately, until now there hasn't been a lot of information about how to successfully invest in these smaller, less known companies. In this book, I share with you my simple system for successfully finding great small-cap stocks for maximum profits.

Contrary to what most people think, small caps as an asset class are relatively safe investments. Over the long term, small caps have outperformed every other class of investments, as I'll show you in a later chapter. And the fact that these investments outperform over the long term makes them a no-brainer for every portfolio. For investors seeking big long-term gains, small caps should be thought of as the home run hitter, the investments that can really help improve overall portfolio returns from average to extraordinary. While the volatility of an individual small-cap stock can be significant, a diversified portfolio of individual stocks, index funds, or mutual funds is

1

recommended for most investors. I believe small caps have a place in every equity investment portfolio, regardless of your investing time horizon.

Throughout this book, I share my investment process and the systems that are involved, and clearly outline the easy steps you need to take to begin uncovering great small-cap gems today. If you seek growth in your portfolio, small caps offer an effective solution. This book shows you how to not only find the winners, but also how to avoid the losers. This is particularly important for investors who experienced significant losses in the stock market crash of 2008 and are looking to aggressively grow their investment portfolio to make up for early losses.

Many investors are skeptical of investment advice from someone who isn't a hedge fund or mutual fund manager. But after the recent collapse of many hedge funds, and under-performance of most mutual funds, being a "money manager" doesn't hold the same prestige that it once did. I often get asked, "If you're such a great investor, why are you selling your information, strategies, and stock picks to individual investors like me?" This is a valid question.

I have never worked for anyone else, but instead have always chosen to do my own thing and taken the path less traveled. This started with my own freelance web design at age 15; the money I earned was invested in the stock market. I started the web site BizFN.com in 1998 while in high school and built it into a leading investment site with content from dozens of investment experts and financial advisors. I attended college for a year before moving on to pursue my entrepreneurial interests. In 2001, I started my Internet publishing company, Business Financial Publishing, which grew to more than $7 million in annual sales within six years, placing my company at number 185 on the *Inc. Magazine* 2008 Inc. 500 list of the fastest-growing private companies in the United States. Prominent accounting firm Deloitte and Touche also selected my company as one of its fastest-growth companies, rating Business Financial Publishing number 66 on its Fast 500 list of high growth private companies in 2008. Today more than one million individual investors receive my updates and insights into the stock market every day through my various investment publications and services including SmallCapInvestor.com.

I've never been a suit-and-tie type of guy and never wanted to have a boss. While my job may not be as prestigious as that of an investment banker or mutual fund manager, it is perfect for me, giving me complete flexibility to spend my time as I choose. Being the boss and owner of my company also allows me to personally invest in great small-cap stocks, educating individual investors, and sharing my top stock picks with others. In a big investment firm, I simply wouldn't have the same flexibility. Running my own company satisfies my passion for small-cap stocks and my desire to share my investing strategies that have worked so well for me. I enjoy helping investors successfully buy great companies at bargain prices before Wall Street and Main Street catch on to these success stories.

Let me tell you how I got started investing at a young age. In 1982, when I was two years old, my grandfather gave each of his grandchildren $1,000 of Exxon stock and signed each of us up for the company's dividend reinvestment plan. Within nine years the shares had appreciated more than 500 percent to $7.50 per share from a split-adjusted $1.20. By age 11, I was sitting on an investment portfolio worth more than $10,000, all in Exxon stock, thanks to my generous grandparents.

On family trips, my parents reminded me that I owned a small piece of every Exxon gas station we passed. While on a family vacation when I was 12, I bought my siblings and cousins ice cream using proceeds from a recent dividend check. No work, and I was able to spend money from the earnings of my investment. This ownership concept sparked my interest in stocks and investments. Before my 12th birthday, my parents helped me set up a discount brokerage account at Charles Schwab.

After liquidating half of my Exxon position, I started having some fun buying more stocks. Some of my first purchases were unknown small caps, including a Midwestern radio media company, a maker of stereo speakers, and a chemicals company. I also bought better-known companies whose brands I was familiar with, like the baseball card company Topps and the candy company Tootsie Roll.

One of my best purchases was a company named Fastenal (Nasdaq: FAST), based in Winona, Minnesota. As an aspiring entrepreneur whose business pursuits included a paper route, I was lucky to deliver the daily newspaper and become friends with Bob, a financial advisor at Robert W. Baird, a Milwaukee-based full-service brokerage firm and the first broker to cover Fastenal. Bob turned me on to this unknown small-cap gem, and together we rode the stock for years and enjoyed lavish gains and consistent profits.

Fastenal was a leading seller of industrial and construction materials, including screws, nuts, and bolts. In the mid-1990s, the company was reporting consistent growth. This was far from a sexy business or a company that was of interest to kids in America; it wasn't Six Flags, Disney, Coke, or Wrigley's.

But Fastenal was a cash machine. And the stock price soared as the company expanded across the country. I began buying the stock in 1993 around a split-adjusted price of $2.50. In 1992, the company's sales were $81.3 million and earnings were $8.8 million. A decade later, the stock price was around $17, and the company was a booming success, with sales of $905 million and earnings of $75 million. Who knew the boring business of nuts and bolts could be so profitable? By the time I cashed out of Fastenal in the late 1990s, my gains were more than 500 percent.

Shares were trading at $36 by the beginning of 2008. Had I continued to hold shares of Fastenal in my portfolio, I would have been sitting on even more impressive gains of 1,340 percent! It is difficult to time the peak price of a stock, and almost impossible to sell at the market top (or buy at the market bottom, for that matter). The key point is that only by selling a stock will you be able to lock in profits. Many investments rise and fall in price, and the prudent investors who make money are those that are willing to sell winners and lock in profits, even though the investment may continue an upward trajectory. But selling out too early can be a common mistake of individual investors. It is important to actively monitor and review every investment in a portfolio, and it is okay to continue to hold winners so long as the investment thesis and fundamentals hold up. At the same time, locking in profits along the way is a good approach to take, even if that means selling only a portion of an investment.

After my Fastenal experience, I was hooked on small caps. Nowhere else could I find stocks capable of such impressive movements in a short period of time. Large-cap stocks just couldn't make such big moves so quickly. How many large caps can gain 500 percent in a few short years? I realized that with small-cap stocks, with a lot of research and a little luck, I could find great undiscovered stocks that were being overlooked by big institutional investors and analysts.

During the 1990s, as a kid growing up in Beloit, Wisconsin, I bought and sold positions in several stocks, some winners and some losers. I began reading the *Wall Street Journal* book series on investing, talking with family friends about their investments, and reading *Barron's Weekly*. I was hooked on investing, utilizing funds from my paper route and other entrepreneurial pursuits to feed my investing habit. I even spent a summer internship working at the Baird branch office in Beloit and at market-making firm Rock Island Securities on the Chicago Stock Exchange to learn more about the stock market from professional asset managers and traders.

I had become an investing junkie by age 15. I spent much of my free time reading books about the investing greats like Warren Buffett and Peter Lynch, digesting investment magazines, reading annual reports from public companies, and digging through press releases and financial information on my dial-up Internet connection at home. I also began reading and participating in online message boards, sharing my opinions with other investors.

I've been an active investor for nearly two-thirds of my life, and as of 2009 I hadn't yet hit age 30. I've been through the dot-com boom of the late 1990s, and the subsequent bust of 2000. I've seen oil soar from $23 a barrel in 2001 to $147 in July 2008, before collapsing to $35 a barrel by the end of the same year. I've seen housing prices (and the share prices of home builders and mortgage companies) jump in the first half of this decade, only to plunge as bad subprime mortgages and poor lending practices tore apart the housing sector and brought the global economy to a screeching halt. During these years, small-cap stocks as a whole fluctuated greatly as measured by the Russell 2000, the index fund serving as the barometer for small-cap stocks. But the thing about small-cap stocks is that there are always winners, in good markets and bad.

There is no shortage of young, innovative public companies doing things differently, and overcoming the challenges facing our society through new solutions, products, and services. This has been true in the two decades that I have been investing and for many decades before that. And it will be true for decades to come.

All of the great large-cap companies that we consider the epitome of success started out as small-cap stocks at some point. Cisco, Dell, Microsoft, and Wal-Mart are the all-time success stories of the stock market. All started small and grew to become the behemoths that they are today. And the early investors who bought these great companies in their infancy stood to profit handsomely as these companies continued to expand year after year.

Every investor I speak with has a story of the small-cap-turned-giant-success that they missed buying, the one that got away.

One of the best reasons to buy small-cap stocks is because others cannot. Most mutual funds and hedge funds simply won't include these stocks in their portfolios. These funds have too much capital to invest, and small-cap stocks are too small for them to purchase without bidding up the share prices or taking on a position that would result in too much exposure to a single company. It isn't that these fund managers dislike small caps; in fact, many of them find these stocks attractive, but they are just too small.

A typical mutual fund might hold 100 stocks in its portfolio. If the fund has $1 billion under management, that translates to an average position of $10 million per stock. In small-cap land, a $10 million position is pretty significant. That translates into a 5 percent stake in a company with a $200 million market cap. Not only is this a large portion of the pie; it also takes too long to buy or sell that much stock, perhaps several months. Because small caps are unknown and there are fewer shares outstanding, share volume in the market is also small. Therefore, the fund can't just go out and buy or sell millions of dollars in stock in a few days. It takes time to build and liquidate positions, increasing the risk for these funds.

Instead of investing in small caps, funds focus on the larger companies mentioned on CNBC and Fox Business News every day, written about in the *Wall Street Journal*, *Fortune*, and *Forbes*, and constantly discussed on Internet message boards and blogs. They'll start buying up the most popular small caps once they have proven themselves and are on the verge of going to mid- or large-cap status, but by then the major profits have already been made by the astute early-stage investors.

This reality points out a problem and also an opportunity. Consider the case of 2008. The financial crisis that year wreaked havoc on the stock market, and caused billions of dollars in losses for investors and future retirees in the United States and around the world. My portfolio also took a beating, especially since I previously owned some index funds for diversification purposes in my retirement accounts, including the Russell 2000 and Russell Micro Cap. These indices track the movements of small- and micro-cap stocks, and their values cratered in 2008, along with all of the other major indices. While some great companies suffered in that economic environment, even those with strong earnings and bright prospects saw their share prices drop significantly as investors sold everything, including the good, the bad, and the ugly.

Small cap stocks took a beating along with every other class of equities. Stocks were trading at rock-bottom prices based on price-to-earnings ratios. The P/E ratio—price per share divided by earnings per share—is one of the most important measures of a company's earning trend over time. I will explain this in detail in a coming chapter. With the Russell 2000 index of small-cap stocks plunging 60 percent from October 2007 to March of 2009, value investors argued that the decline in stocks had created a "generational low" price for stocks, and a buying opportunity for brave investors.

Investors benefit by focusing on growth when markets have fallen. Buying municipal bonds, T-bills, and other conservative debt instruments will not bring an investment portfolio back from the brink of extinction. It may preserve capital, but it won't make up for significant losses. To recover, you need to take an intelligent equity-based approach.

Small caps benefit a portfolio and can be represented in every diversified portfolio hoping to generate capital gains. History has shown that small-cap stocks are among the most attractive investments after a financial downturn.

The great small caps, the ones I will show you how to find, are agile, opportunistic businesses that thrive in good times and bad. These companies and their leaders seize upon opportunities to create profits regardless of the environment. They have fewer employees, smaller overhead, greater financial incentives for their employees, and aren't burdened by big pension plans, like those of General Motors, that weigh on the entire company. Given their nimble nature, small caps can retool and address market opportunities more quickly and efficiently than larger behemoths that take forever to make even small changes. These are the companies that I seek to buy and the ones that will perform best over time.

I love to take risks. This should come as no surprise. I've always been a risk taker with my entrepreneurial companies and my investments. My game in Las Vegas is blackjack. I can sit for hours at a card table, watching the cards and making value judgments about my odds. I find that small-cap investing can be as fun as blackjack in Vegas, but your odds are much better if you do your homework. Playing blackjack, the casino has an average of 0.5 percent edge (varying by the number of decks being used) if the player is using basic strategy. That makes blackjack the most profitable of all Las Vegas games for the player, and if you vary your bets properly, you can even win occasionally.

With small-cap stocks, your advantage of winning is even better, as are the profits from those winning positions. By using my methodical process to pick stocks and time buy and sell decisions, you'll have a huge edge over other investors and book major profits. In blackjack, a typical winning hand results in a payout equal to your bet, or the equivalent of a 100 percent return. But with stocks, the upside potential is much greater.

My goal with this book is to help you find the next great small-cap stock that could become the Cisco, Dell, Microsoft, or Wal-Mart of tomorrow. None of these large-cap companies will see their shares multiply by a factor of 10 in the next decade. But dozens of small-cap stocks will see their shares achieve 10-bagger status, to borrow Peter Lynch's term for stocks that appreciate by +1,000 percent.

I believe in my own process and use it every day. I am going to show you how to find the next unknown sleeper that could become your own goldmine.

CHAPTER 1

Start Small, Finish Big—Discover Big Profits in Small-Cap Stocks

"If I was running $1 million today, or $10 million for that matter, I'd be fully invested. Anyone who says that size does not hurt investment performance is selling. The highest rates of return I've ever achieved were in the 1950s. I killed the Dow. You ought to see the numbers. But I was investing peanuts then. It's a huge structural advantage not to have a lot of money. I think I could make you 50 percent a year on $1 million. No, I know I could. I guarantee that.

The universe I can't play in has become more attractive than the universe I can play in. I have to look for elephants. It may be that the elephants are not as attractive as the mosquitoes. But that is the universe I must live in."
—Warren Buffett, 1999, discussing small-cap stocks

An old saying claims that big shots are the little shots who just keep shooting.

In the case of the stock market—in particular, the world of small-cap stocks—that maxim is decidedly true. And that is terrific news for *you*. Over the last decade, I've developed a system for consistently finding outstanding small-cap stocks that deliver big gains to early investors. Throughout this book, I'll share everything you need to know to achieve similar results in your own investment portfolio.

All great companies start out small. They are built by entrepreneurs who invest their time and money, raise capital privately, and turn their dreams into reality. Many of the world's greatest innovations come from small, entrepreneurial companies, and very few come from the behemoths. In recent decades, smaller companies have increasingly been investing in research and development, helping fuel the growth of the overall economy. To illustrate: In 1981, 71 percent of corporate research and development dollars in the United States was spent by companies with more than 25,000 employees, while companies with fewer than 1,000 employees spent just 4 percent. By 2006, the large companies' share had dropped to 38 percent, while the small companies' share had risen to 23.7 percent; it is a trend that has continued to shift.[1]

Why? Charles Matthews, executive director of the Center for Entrepreneurship Education and Research at the University of Cincinnati, has observed that smaller firms historically employ a large percentage of computer analysts, engineers, and scientists. This drives an interest in innovation and research; today, most new jobs are generated among small companies, where the growth rate is going to be rapid in comparison to their larger competitors.

Small businesses are excellent incubators of innovation, especially technology-driven innovation. With generally flatter organizational structures, these leaner, hungrier companies can cut through the red tape, remain focused, and drive innovation with passion and efficiency.

The best of these young, innovative companies become publicly traded small-cap stocks. This allows individual investors like you to buy a piece of the action, and participate in the future growth and profits of these companies.

Small-Cap Investor: Eight-Step Process for Big Profits from Small Stocks

Throughout this book, I share with you my eight-step system for finding great small-cap stocks with big potential for financial out-performance and share price gains. I will show you exactly what you need to do to become a small-cap guru and profitable investor in small-cap stocks.

There are eight simple steps to follow in order to find, research, and analyze small-cap stocks that could put big gains in your portfolio.

Step 1: *Growth Trends:* Identify growth trends and market sectors positioned for rapid growth in the years to come.

Step 2: *Finding Potential Winners:* Screen more than 7,000 publicly traded companies to find those companies that are unknown performers positioned to grow.

Step 3: *Fundamentals Matter:* Understand the fundamentals of the potential investment, including products, services, and management's ability to run the business.

Step 4: *Financial Performance:* Review and evaluate key metrics in a company's financial statements to understand historical financial performance.

Step 5: *Earnings Quality:* Look for red flags that indicate financial manipulation or fraud to avoid investing in a small-cap lemon.

Step 6: *Growth Outlook:* Develop an understanding of expectations for growth to make valid valuation comparisons.

Step 7: *Technical Analysis:* Understand the technical indicators of share price movements to help timing of investments, and maximize profits while limiting losses.

Step 8: *Pulling the Trigger:* Determine the optimal timing for entering new positions by using effective trading strategies.

Using my system for finding, researching, analyzing, and ultimately buying and selling small-cap stocks will make it easy for you to find those companies with huge potential upside, and determine when and how to maximize your profits.

Throughout the book, I show you exactly how to use these eight simple steps for consistently finding and profiting from great small-cap stocks before their shares take off.

Small Caps as Generators of Growth

Many of the smaller, innovative growth companies that are publicly traded fit the definition of small caps. Market capitalization is a measure of the total value of a company, calculated by multiplying shares outstanding by share price. As the term "small cap" suggests, these are the smaller companies, those with a market capitalization below $2 billion (mid caps range in size between $2 billion and $10 billion, and large caps are those with market caps exceeding $10 billion).

On my investment website, SmallCapInvestor.com, I focus on the small-cap stocks with market capitalization *below* $2 billion, and often those below $500 million. It is often the case that the smaller the better when trying to find companies poised to deliver big gains. Table 1.1 shows a list of the 10 best performing stocks and their returns for the decade ending December 31, 2007.

The returns are impressive. But look at the market capitalizations of these companies in 1998; nearly all of them are below $100 million. The smallest of the small caps tend to perform best—those unknown gems that have not yet become the darlings of Wall Street.

How many of these companies had you heard of in 1998, or even today after their significant growth? With the exception of Apple, probably not many. This is because most of the best small-cap opportunities are not well known today, and the key is to find them right before they become huge successes and their shares have risen significantly. This is the challenge.

TABLE 1.1   Top 10 Best Performing Stocks: 1998–2007

Company	Jan. 1, 1998 Market Cap	Dec. 31, 2007 Market Cap	Return 1998–2007
Hansen Natural (Nasdaq: HANS)	$16.5 million	$3.83 billion	21,201%
Asta Funding (Nasdaq: ASFI)	$3.1 million	$326.3 million	8,252%
Celgene (Nasdaq: CELG)	$129.0 million	$22.74 billion	6,771%
Apple (Nasdaq: AAPL)	$1.7 billion	$176.4 billion	5,959%
Comtech Telecommunications (Nasdaq: CMTL)	$11.3 million	$1.34 billion	4,246%
Daktronics (Nasdaq: DAKT)	$23.1 million	$917.4 million	3,493%
Green Mountain Coffee Roasters (Nasdaq: GMCR)	$24.7 million	$1.0 billion	3,455%
Clean Harbors (CLH)	$15.8 million	$1.23 billion	3,378%
Innodata Isogen (INOD)	$3.1 million	$128.9 million	3,135%
Immucor (BLUD)	$70.0 million	$2.39 billion	2,941%

Source: Capital IQ, www.capitaliq.com

What is most appealing about small-cap stocks? There are a number of attributes. An investment-worthy small cap is often a young company experiencing its fastest period of growth. The company introduces new products or services, launches strategic partnerships, or enters a new market while still flying under the radar of its larger competitors, remaining unnoticed by Wall Street analysts and investors. With fewer employees and lower expenses compared with larger companies, small caps have the unrestrained flexibility to pursue growth and have the ability and desire to take risks that are often avoided by the dominant industry players. This situation can catapult a small, unknown company into a roaring success, and in doing so, create millionaires out of early shareholders who stay the course.

Want proof? Let's examine a few examples of some of the best performing stocks in the history of the stock market. While I'm sure you're familiar with each of these companies, perhaps you are less aware that all started as entrepreneurial, small-cap companies that grew into well-known businesses, making big gains for early investors:

- *Cisco Systems* (Nasdaq: CSCO): An investment of $10,000 in 1990 grew to $34.5 million by 2008, a gain of over 34,000 percent. The company's IPO valued the tech company at $224 million, and 18 years later the company was valued at $180 billion. The reason that Cisco has grown in an explosive arc is due to yet another trend identified early and ridden from there on: computer networking. The brainchild of husband and wife Len Bosack and Sandy Lerner, the company got its start by developing and selling routers, but not just any other router like those already on the market. Theirs was the first to support multiple network protocols; although that technology was eventually supplanted, Cisco had its foothold. The company later branched out with careful insight, moving into Ethernet, switching, security, ATM networking, and other areas. Although Cisco was, in fact, the most valuable company in the world at the peak of the dot-com boom of the late 1990s and into the early 21st Century, it has since declined in value but remains one of the icons of the American technology community.

- *Dell* (Nasdaq: DELL): went public in June 1988 as a small-cap valued at $200 million. As of the end of 2008, market cap was more than $20 billion. An investment of $10,000 in June 1988 grew to $2.8 million in 20 years. Why the meteoric rise? The most revolutionary aspect of Dell's operation was its direct sales marketing strategy. Rather than using resellers to sell its products, Dell established a one-on-one relationship with its customers. But that meant more than just direct selling. It spelled the beginning of a highly personal form of interaction with Dell customers. For instance, in 1985 Dell began establishing customer service as the bedrock of the company's philosophy and approach, offering a risk-free return policy and next day in-home professional support. Three years later, Dell raised $30 million in its initial public offering, and the company was off and running.
- *Microsoft* (Nasdaq: MSFT): An investment of $10,000 in 1986 was worth $3.4 million by 2008, as the company's market capitalization soared from $488 million at the time of its IPO to over $200 billion. An idea whose time had come—the personal computer in every household—quickly established Microsoft as the premier provider of user-friendly software. Although the company is now synonymous with its line of Windows products, its first real commercial success derived from its DOS operating systems (remember those?). Microsoft beat out IBM because its Windows system was simply easier to use—in fact, much easier. The company debuted in the public market with a share price of $21. Thanks to these and other innovations, by December 1999 the price per share (adjusted for stock splits) topped over $17,000.
- *Wal-Mart* (NYSE: WMT): An investment of $10,000 in 1972 was worth $7.61 million by 2008. Like other small companies that blossomed, Wal-Mart captured and leveraged a revolutionary idea—in Wal-Mart's case, discount retailing. The company went public with a market capitalization of only $21 million, and it was worth $200 billion by 2008. Prior to opening his first store in Rogers, Arkansas, in 1962, Sam Walton exhaustively researched the prevailing consumer market and determined that shoppers could live better by saving on a broad variety of goods and products. For Walton, that was in large part a bottom-up proposition;

as the company grew, Walton still tried to visit each store at least once a year, asking employees for their input and singular perspective of what consumers wanted and valued most. (This direct market research style is employed by Starbucks founder Howard Schultz and other retail executives.)

Although Wal-Mart has come under fire for labor practices and other issues, its success is undeniable. By 2009, 7,390 Wal-Mart stores (and its adjunct Sam's Club operations) were open for business, employing more than two million people and making the company the largest retailer and private employer in the world.

These are all extraordinary success stories, but they're by no means exceptions to the rule, particularly when you look at the long term. While these are the big name winners that every investor aspires to duplicate with his or her investments, buying Cisco Systems in 1990 and holding it until today isn't the norm. But for every Cisco Systems or Microsoft, there are hundreds of lesser-known small-cap companies providing early investors with gains of 100, 300, 500, and even more than 1,000 percent. Even if the company doesn't become a household name, investors can bank major gains from the appreciation in share price. And the best part is that most people, active investors included, have never heard of many of these companies, even after they have posted huge returns. Table 1.2 identifies some of these lesser-known success stories over the past five years.

Small-cap stocks fit nicely into just about anyone's investment portfolio. No matter if you're in your twenties, saving for your children's college education, or currently retired, small caps have a place in a well-diversified plan, along with mid- and large-cap equities and fixed income securities. The growth that can be achieved with small-cap stocks is significant, and can help boost the returns for a diversified portfolio. For this reason alone, small caps must be on the table for every investor.

TABLE 1.2   Top Five Best Performing Stocks: 2003 to 2008

Company	Share Price December 31, 2003	Share Price December 31, 2008	Five-Year Gain
Terra Industries (NYSE: TRA)	$2.48	$21.12	751%
Cleveland-Cliffs (NYSE: CLF)	$3.59	$27.19	657%
ViroPharma (Nasdaq: VPHM)	$2.89	$11.31	291%
PetroQuest (NYSE: PQ)	$2.30	$ 8.53	270%
AspenBio Pharma (Nasdaq: APPY)	$1.40	$ 4.80	242%

Source: The Motley Fool, www.fool.com

An Example of Small-Cap Success

The companies highlighted in the previous section make my point that finding the great small-cap companies before they take off is a profitable venture. Figure 1.1 shows an example of another small cap that I tracked, culminating in a decision to alert my subscribers to the opportunity.

I am sure you have never heard of Almost Family Inc. (Nasdaq: AFAM). Almost Family provides in-home health care services in nine states (Florida, Kentucky, Ohio, Connecticut, Massachusetts, Alabama, Indiana, Illinois, and Missouri), bypassing nursing homes and other facilities that most elderly individuals and their families would rather not use. Almost Family has experienced extraordinary gains in share price. Have a look at how the company's stock trended from 2004 to the latter part of 2008.

This growth is attributed to several key factors, primarily structuring services to suit a carefully tailored market. From 2003 through 2007, sales rose dramatically from $59.5 million to $132.1 million, an increase of 122 percent. Over the same period, earnings per share (EPS) soared from $0.02 to $1.40. As the aging of America continues—with increasing numbers of the population living to an older age and Baby Boomers approaching their retirement years—the need for comprehensive elder care has never been so critical.

The combination is a powerful one, a growing trend met by a personal option that allows the elderly to remain in their homes and, in effect, recognition of both a nationwide pattern and the emotional appeal of this approach. As a result of this attractive marketing of services, Almost Family was named number 24 in the *Forbes* ranking of the best small companies in America in 2008.

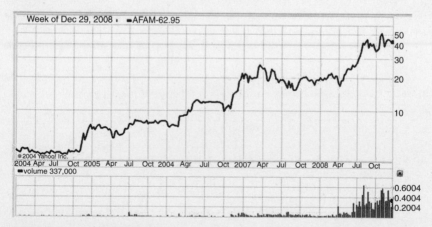

FIGURE 1.1   Almost Family Inc.
Source: Yahoo! Inc.

Almost Family has been in business for many years. However, many great small-cap companies are young and don't have decades of financial history. It is most important to take the data available and evaluate it to determine the company's performance. The financial performance from the past few quarters or year will provide a much better understanding of the current performance and outlook for the future than financial performance from 10 years ago. After all, our investments are really a bet on the future of a company and not the past. Certainly, historical financial results must be examined when trying to predict the future, but the basis of all investments must be forward thinking, not backward looking. Almost Family's stellar financial performance even during a challenging economic period demonstrates the company's strong business model and resilience.

Ned Davis Research, an investment research firm, reported in 2008 that "small-cap stocks tend to significantly begin outperforming large-cap stocks at about the same time and typically continue leading for at least a year after the recession has ended." The same study observed that in a one-year period after the last nine recessions, small caps yielded an average of 24 percent return, versus less than 18 percent from the S&P 500.[2]

It is helpful to consider the long-term performance of small caps over time to understand how this class of equities can benefit long-term investors. To illustrate that point, look at Figure 1.2, comparing returns of five asset classes: U.S. Treasury bills, long-term government bonds, corporate bonds, equity returns from larger stocks on the New York and American stock exchanges, and small stocks. Figure 1.2 assumes that $1 was invested in December 1925 and that all proceeds were reinvested.

This research from Duke University indicates that over the long-term, small-cap stocks outperform all other investment classes. From December 1925 to June 1995, small caps led the way: $1 invested in small caps grew to $3,425 during this period. $1 invested in the next best performing investment—the S&P Total Return, representing large-cap stocks—grew to just $973.

Figure 1.3 is the annual chart showing the cumulative returns (for $1 invested, and with dividends reinvested) of large caps and small caps from 1926 to 2004.

Figure 1.3 reveals two significant facts:

1. Small caps have outperformed large caps by a 5-to-1 ratio since 1926, especially over the last 40 years. This "size effect" is significant; not all of the excess returns can be explained by the higher risk in buying shares of small-cap companies.
2. From 1926 to 1957, small caps underperformed large caps on a consistent basis. Throughout the 1920s, many U.S. investors were willing to buy shares of small- and mid-sized companies believing that they

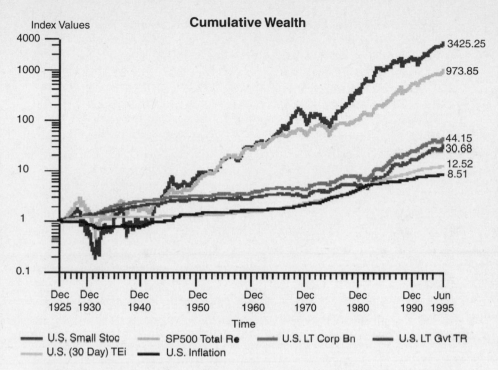

FIGURE 1.2   Cumulative Wealth 1925 to 1995: U.S. Small-Cap Stocks Outperform Other Asset Classes

Source: Duke University

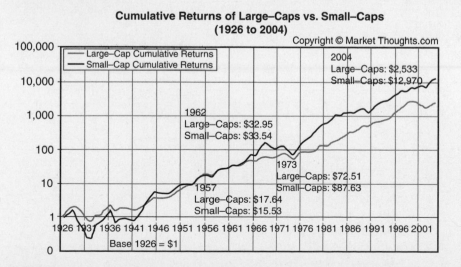

FIGURE 1.3   Cumulative Returns of Large Caps vs. Small Caps (1926 to 2004)

Source: Copyright © 2009 MarketThoughts LLC

could sustain themselves as well as large-sized companies during economic recessions. The huge bear market and subsequent Depression from September 1929 to July 1932 dispelled that belief, and for the next 30 years, investors refused to buy shares of small caps unless they were trading at deep discounts to shares of large-cap companies. More stringent reporting requirements by the SEC after the 1929–1932 crash did much to improve the quality of smaller companies listed on the NYSE, and provided investors with the information needed in order for them to determine whether the stocks were sound.

It may be reasonable to believe that an intelligent investor can simply put money in small-cap index funds and forget about their investment until retirement. But this strategy may not be wise, as small cap out-performance has also been mired in bull and bear markets since 1926. For example, large caps outperformed small caps from 1926 to 1931. They beat small caps again from 1946 to 1948, and again (with the exception of 1954) from 1951 to 1957. Just as stocks have outperformed bonds on a long-term basis but underperformed for significant periods of time, it is not a given that small caps will outperform large caps every year. Table 1.3 is an illustration of historical periods where small caps have outperformed large caps consistently.

Indices are designed to yield average returns. If you buy the Dow Jones Industrial Average index, and the stock market moves higher, it's a safe bet that the Dow will move in-line with the overall move of the stock market. However, investing in indices isn't a good option for investors looking to beat the market. For investors seeking above average returns, individual stocks are the way to go.

TABLE 1.3   Periods of Small Cap Outperformance in the U.S.

Periods	Duration (Years)	Outperformance (%)
1932 to 1934	3	105
1938 to 1945	8	224
1949 to 1950	2	6
1958 to 1959	2	20
1963 to 1968	6	152
1974 to 1983	10	344
1991 to 1994	4	42
1999 to 2004	6	135
Average	5.13	129

Source: Ibbotson (SSBI Yearbook)

The Russell Investment Group manages several well-known indices, including the Russell 2000 and Russell MicroCap, which serve as barometers for small-cap stocks. Russell has claimed that large caps outperformed small caps from 2005 through 2007. If this is the case, then the 1999 to 2004 period of small caps out-performance ended. Small caps continued to lead the market for several years through the dot-com crash and decline of the market in 2001. As with all investments, no one class of equities can outperform forever. While small caps underperformed compared with large caps from 2005 through 2007, evidence shows that the smaller companies will lead the market coming out of a recession, and that these companies bounce back faster. After the crash of 2008, small caps will lead the way. Regardless of the overall performance of small caps, there are always opportunities for individual investors to find great, profitable, high-growth companies trading at very attractive valuations. And through this book, I provide you with the strategies required to find and profit from these opportunities in good markets and bad.[3]

Small-Cap Value Stocks Outperform Large-Cap Growth Stocks

Between 1926 and 2004, large-cap growth stocks had an average annual return of about 9.26 percent. Accordingly, $10,000 invested in large-cap growth stocks in 1926 would have grown to about $10 million by 2004. That's not too shabby. But this pales when compared to the impressive 15.9 percent *annual return* of small-cap value stocks in the same time period. So $10,000 invested in small-cap value stocks in 1926 would have grown to about $1 billion by 2004.

Figure 1.4 shows a summary of these returns from the *New York Times* in 2008.

The difference between the highest and lowest returns is dramatic. If only we had all bought $10,000 worth of small caps in 1926! Unfortunately, most of us weren't alive at that time, and if we were, we likely didn't have $10,000 and the conviction to buy small caps.

Profitable Small Caps Don't Always Make Gains on Day One

We have seen how small caps historically outperform other investments over the long haul. But buying and holding a small-cap index may not be the best way to generate big returns in your portfolio today. However, investing in a selective group of individual stocks poised for rapid growth and trading at attractive valuations can deliver big gains and improve the total return for your investment portfolio.

Smaller and More Rewarding

Since 1926, the average small-cap value stock
has significantly outperformed the average large-cap
growth stock.

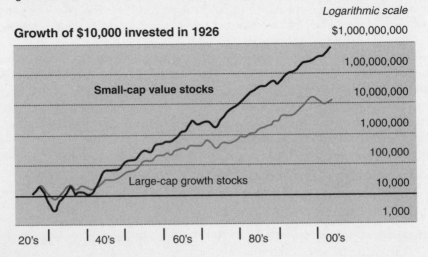

FIGURE 1.4   Smaller and More Rewarding

Source: The New York Times

Let's go back to an individual stock example. Small-cap success is not
exclusively the story of companies starting out small and getting bigger.
Many equally appealing examples involve turning around a bad situation
and creating a new direction.

In other words, small-cap successes are not limited to companies that
started small and took off from the day they went public. There are plenty
of successful turnarounds as well—companies that fell on hard times, only
to recover under the leadership of a new team or with a different business direction or strategy. Bankrate Inc. (Nasdaq: RATE) is one example.
Bankrate.com is a leading website for consumers seeking information about
loans, including home and auto loans, and credit cards. Bankrate went public in May 1999 at $12 per share.

Along with other Internet stocks that dropped like rocks with the dot-
com crash of 2000, by the end of 2001, shares had lost 95 percent of their
value, plummeting to 65 cents a share. Former Bloomberg L.P. executive
Elisabeth DeMarse was brought in to turn the company around in 2000,
but the stock languished for two more years. It was during this time that I
discovered BankRate. The company was cash flow positive, had a market

cap of $15 million, $8 million in cash in the bank, no debt, and growing revenues and earnings. I presented the stock to subscribers of my small-cap newsletter service when shares were trading at $1.05 in July 2002.

The company then started reporting a long string of positive financial results; having lost nearly $17 million in 2000, the company reported a net profit of nearly $7 million just two years later. The stock made astounding gains. Shares increased over 5,000 percent between 2002 and 2008. By 2008, Bankrate's market cap had grown to $700 million. The stock ultimately went as high as $55 in 2008, an increase of 5,138 percent in six years.

Even though Bankrate struggled for a time, it hit on a formula that promised long-term success: personalized financing information, which paralleled an increase in loan requests as a result of the housing and refinancing boom and increased Internet advertising in the financial services sector. Rather than having to call banks and complete multiple loan applications, Bankrate became a one-stop shopping destination on the Web for individuals seeking home loans, car loans, or refinancing. In this case, the key to success was tapping into multiple growth trends—increased consumer borrowing coupled with growing online advertising spending.

Small-cap companies are up for grabs, and individual investors doing their homework often will find excellent investments not yet widely recognized by the smart money crowd on Wall Street. Small caps are where Main Street investors like you and me can enjoy extraordinary returns.

Bigger Gains from Low-Priced Stocks

It is important to differentiate between small-cap stocks and low-priced or penny stocks. Market capitalization is simply a calculation of the current market value of a company, and it uses share price to calculate one half of the equation. Stocks with low share prices typically have smaller market cap, but this isn't always the case. For example, consider Citigroup (NYSE: C), market cap $17 billion, share price early in 2009 of $3; Taiwan Demiconductor (NYSE: TSM), market cap $43 billion, share price $7. The SEC defines *penny stocks* as those companies with share prices below $5. Most of these are small-cap or micro-cap stocks.

Because small-cap stocks are often thinly traded (meaning fewer shares traded every day), even modest buying can move a company's share price quickly. And, because share price is often quite low, a $1 increase in the price of a small-cap stock often represents a much higher percentage gain than a similar shift in its larger brethren. When investing in stocks, it's all about banking big percentage gains and limiting losses. For example, a $1 price increase in a stock trading at $6 per share is a gain of almost 17 percent. The same price increase for a $50 stock is a gain of only 2 percent.

The surprising thing is that it's easier to find these stocks than you might think. Young companies are much more likely to create or take advantage of new trends in the marketplace and are more opportunistic. Just by looking at changing trends in recent years, such as the Internet, the iPod craze, and the soaring demand for alternative energy sources like solar power, investors can find great companies that will benefit from these developments. Small-cap stocks targeting these trends will financially reward those astute investors who pony up their chips while others continue to seek investments with certainty in an uncertain world.

Innovations are part of the reason small-cap companies are exciting; changing technology is another. At the beginning of the 20th Century, many people anticipated automobile or air travel advances, adding to a field of amazing new ideas, all creating new industries. Now, 100 years later, the world is a rapidly changing one. Old industries are going obsolete (when was the last time you needed to shoe your horse or, for that matter, drop off a roll of film to be developed?).

So what's the potential downside of small caps? The world economy was in flux from 2007 to 2009. The latter part of that period saw the largest prolonged drop in the stock market since The Great Depression, and no one could anticipate the next rise or fall, its extent, or its duration. Economic cycles are inevitable, but their timing and severity can never be known in advance. This is the elephant in the room that is too often ignored. Why? Because the market tends to be euphoric in good times and suicidal in bad times. It is like an ill-adjusted person, subject to extreme moods and rarely level-headed.

Remember, though, that even the most sobering time is also a time of extraordinary opportunity. Stocks—and, in particular, small-cap stocks—are at bargain prices when markets drop, especially to the extremes of 2008 and early 2009. Given that I'm an unabashed fan of small-cap stocks—and have enjoyed significant success in the recommendations I've shared with my subscribers—I have total confidence that small caps are most likely to lead the way to recovery after a bear market. This has been the case with corrections following a bear market in the past, and I believe the same will be true in the future.

However, since small-cap stocks are intrinsically more volatile, you also need to exercise extra care in examining their fundamentals. Small caps' higher relative volatility stems from their relatively low liquidity. This means there are fewer shares available to buy or sell on the open market compared to larger companies, so small caps can move fast, even on relatively small pieces of information or news. For the savvy and well-researched investor, this can mean quick and sizable gains; for those who fail to do adequate legwork, steep losses can just as easily be the result.

With less coverage from analysts, institutional investors, and the financial media, many small caps fly under the radar. This can be good for small-cap investors, as it provides opportunities. But it also means that most small caps go unchecked, without the coverage and exposure that exposes potential problems for investors. For this reason, thorough research is an absolute requirement for successful small-cap investing.

Many low-quality companies trade on the "pink sheets," an electronic exchange that is largely unregulated and considered the Wild Wild West for investing. Stocks listed there are often of suspect quality, as these companies may not be required to report financial results to the Securities and Exchange Commission (SEC). That can make it virtually impossible for investors to determine the value of the firm or its underlying stock. And even the OTC Bulletin Board (OTC BB), which requires companies to file timely financial statements with the SEC, can be littered with shell companies and "pump and dump" stock shams. While there are some great opportunities with OTC BB companies, avoiding pink sheet stocks is a wise decision for those looking to invest, rather than gamble, in the stock market.

Pump and Dump

"Pump and dump" is an illegal activity and a common form of stock manipulation. Here's how it takes place: Someone with a position in a stock promotes the company's value (pumps), often in an investment chat room or message board. If this succeeds and many more people buy the stock, the original investor then sells shares (dumps) at a profit. This works well with small caps because the number of shares is relatively limited, meaning even a small change in volume can make a big difference in the share price.

You also need to be diligent even with companies required to report their financials. Since small, fast-growing companies are often under pressure to maintain earnings growth, they can be prone to manipulate financial statements to make financial conditions look better than they actually are. Ultimately, not even the most adept financial chicanery can hide the truth; when word gets out that a company's financials are not up to snuff, its stock value can plummet. And when they crash, they crash hard.

The good news is that there are almost always telltale signs that point out either corporate malfeasance or merely bad bookkeeping. Later in this book, I'll go into detail about what to look for in a company's financials, arming you with the skills and knowledge necessary to separate potential winners from other small caps that are more likely to stumble.

Financials are a critical element in small-cap stock analysis. I encourage you to not overlook this aspect of small-cap research. The financials let you see just how well a small cap is performing and how likely it is that it will maintain that sort of performance. The numbers by themselves are only a single entry, but the trend reveals all. Understanding financial statements is key to successful investing, and I will delve into this in detail in a later chapter. First, however, I need to talk about some important theories about how the market works. A variety of different approaches have found their way into the market culture, and we all need to make sure that the method we use for trying to anticipate the direction of the next trend is in fact an *accurate* method. One of the most misleading among the popular theories about the market is the so-called efficient market theory.

The Inefficient Market Theory: The Small-Cap Advantage

The efficient market theory is preferred among academic market experts because it makes the whole thing nice and tidy and easy to predict, even though in the real world far more chaos prevails. The efficient market theory states that all information available publicly is already factored into the price of a stock.

What is wrong with this idea? In reality, chaos dominates the market. Price movement tends to consist of many overreactions in the short term, so that a single day's price movement is going to be corrected the following day (or the following hour). Buyers overreact when the news is good, scooping up shares at inflated prices; sellers overreact on the other side, dumping bargain-priced shares to avoid further losses. At the top of the price trend, greed dominates; at the bottom, the predominant emotion is panic. Among the hundreds of maxims about the market, the one that most accurately dispels the myth of the efficient market theory is this: "Bulls can make money, and bears can make money. But pigs and chickens get slaughtered."

The constant struggle between buyers and sellers, with trades made in the middle of a vast array of information, news, and rumor, demonstrates that in fact the market really operates on the *inefficient* market theory.

Under this more realistic idea, the current price of a stock is the culmination of all known information, *true and false*, and that the overall mood has exaggerated the latest price movement (too far up on good news and too far down on bad news).

The efficient market theory raises many questions, and properly so. Most people can spot a flawed theory right away because their common sense tells them it cannot be so simple. The efficient approach is no exception. Consider these questions:

- Do all investors access the Internet at the same moment?
- Does everyone refer to the same websites for information?
- Do all investors talk to their family, friends, and people in the investment community in absolute lockstep?
- Is it not more likely that two people buying or selling the same stock are naturally going to make those decisions based on differing reasons?
- Can anyone reasonably argue that, if you both decide to buy a particular small-cap stock, you came to that choice based on an identical path of reasoning and information?

Remember, the efficient market theory doesn't claim to be instantly accurate all the time it says that investors have to allow sufficient time for the parity that the hypothesis embraces to level out. That's reasonable, but some stocks that have tumbled take years to recover while others bounce back within a quarter, if not sooner. Where's the parity in that? It's like putting a bag of popcorn in the microwave oven expecting to see every kernel pop in the exact same instance, or at least within a reasonable amount of time. The truth is that some kernels pop sooner, while others pop later. Still others never pop at all.

The Market as an Emotional Being

Another ingredient is the powerful effect of emotion. The stock market in 2008 and 2009 was in the heart of the maelstrom resulting from debate over the bailout of several major financial institutions, ongoing credit problems stemming from subprime mortgage write-offs, and growing unemployment indicating a recession. Here's one headline that topped the business section of a prominent daily newspaper of the time: "Persistent Anxiety over Tight Credit Sends Stocks Plunging." The bedrock of that headline was the word "anxiety." Variations of this theme could be found daily in the fourth quarter of 2008 and beyond.

Investor emotion—particularly with regard to the herd mentality of the market—can move mountains. Of course, that emotion can derive from empirical data, but that's not to suggest that every investor's and institution's gut reaction to the same bit of information is going to be identical. In a sense, that's asking for a far more robotic pattern than humans can ever be expected to follow.

In the interest of being as balanced as possible, there is more truth to the efficient market theory today than when it was first posited some 40 years ago, if only due to the speed and broad access of the Internet. The trouble is, it really has little to do with the hypothesis itself. The explosion of the Internet and the proliferation of computers and portable devices that display information have contributed to the fastest sharing and dissemination of investment news and analysis ever, so in that sense we enjoy the efficient communication theory. Beyond this, we have no more efficiency today than in the past. Markets have always been chaotic and always will be.

Bottom line: In an economy based on perfect information, all participants consistently act in a completely rational fashion.

Go to your favorite Internet financial site. What are the basic elements? Perhaps the Dow Jones Average is careening up or down. Maybe it's news about some giant company announcing layoffs or meeting (or failing to meet) earnings expectations or the financial and economic forecast for an entire nation or region.

Traditional news outlets have only so many resources and space with which to report what they deem to be of significance. When multibillion-dollar behemoths announce important developments, news that is every bit as important to small-cap stocks tends to go by the wayside—or, at the very least, becomes buried in the back pages. The media focus on the most popular companies with the largest followings. These typically are larger companies, given their well-known brands, large market capitalization, and extensive number of shareholders. In the media business, the larger the audience the better, since media companies generate most of their revenues from advertising. For example, Pfizer has 12 analysts following it; by contrast, there are dozens of promising small-cap pharmaceutical firms out there that have little or no analyst coverage. Think of just how quickly media outlets would spread Pfizer-related news versus that of a smaller player. Even today, someone, like myself, who's built a career around investing in small caps still has to proactively seek information on small caps. When it comes to larger firms, the news somehow always finds me.

And this is where you can profit. Do your research, look for news, and buy when the fundamentals and valuation tell you the stock is a winner. If you're an early and immediate buyer, you'll be likely to see a steady increase in your investment value as the news becomes well known by other investors.

While salient investing information is much more accessible than it was even a decade or so ago, accessibility doesn't by definition mean that every individual investor or every institution is going to access it—or, for that matter, treat it and react to it in an identical fashion.

While technology has made information increasingly accessible, the fact remains that it is still human beings who are pushing all those buttons. We see things differently. We react differently. We prioritize information in different ways and with different results. And, we all make mistakes.

As a diligent investor, you want to avoid the mistakes that other investors make, mistakes borne of focusing just on the big news at the expense of less visible data that, when interpreted properly, can result in remarkable investing profit. Taken in concert with the flaws of the efficient market theory, you need to investigate sources of information that point you to those small-cap stocks flying under the radar.

The Bottom Line

- The lion's share of innovation and development now derives from smaller companies.
- Small caps consistently outperform larger companies over the long-term.
- Big stock market winners such as Cisco, Dell, Microsoft, and Wal-Mart all started as entrepreneurial small caps and grew to become huge successes.
- As a small-cap stock investor, you seek the small, fast-growing companies that have yet to be recognized by the mainstream investing community.
- Many of the biggest small-cap winners share the attribute of recognizing a trend or market before others do and building their success on that innovation.
- Even a small increase in the price of a low-priced stock can mean a significant percentage gain.
- Successful investing in small-cap stocks requires thorough research.
- The market for small caps is inefficient, allowing individual investors to gain an edge over large institutional investors.
- Watch for signs among small-cap stocks that suggest positive upcoming news. You have an advantage because small caps are often overlooked by 99 percent of investors.

CHAPTER 2

Big Ideas for Big Profits

"Successful investing is anticipating the anticipations of others."
—John Maynard Keynes

"You do things when the opportunities come along. I've had periods in my life when I've had a bundle of ideas come along, and I've had long dry spells. If I get an idea next week, I'll do something. If not, I won't do a damn thing."

—Warren Buffett

A small cap with rapidly growing revenues, high gross margins, and better results than its competitors is a viable small-cap candidate for your portfolio. My guideline for high-growth companies is growth in revenues and earnings greater than 20 percent per year. These financial strengths make companies exceptionally competitive, so that a relatively young company will be destined to overtake its peers and dominate its industry. Look at the history of Wal-Mart in comparison to the more dismal retail results for Sears. Where Sears once dominated the market, they have been replaced by Wal-Mart, whose growth has continued year in and year out even when the company was quite small and with a limited geographic footprint.

But where do you find these gems? The most obvious place to look for emerging small-cap companies is the financial media—newspapers, magazines, and popular financial web sites. However, these are the worst news sources for generating ideas for your portfolio—investments that you should tune out and ignore.

Ironically, many of the best emerging small-cap stocks remain largely ignored in the mainstream financial press, and by the time they are making headlines and magazine covers, the ideas have already played out and the early profits, which also happen to be the largest, have been captured by astute early-stage investors.

The exposure of media or analysts is self-defeating because it is no longer possible for you to buy shares at attractive valuations that are available before the public has caught wind of a good investment idea. You need to develop other sources for information. Contrarian investing is a strategy for seeking investments that are out of favor with most investors. Contrarian investors aim to invest contrary to others—finding great investment ideas, themes, and trends before they are accepted and thought to be smart investments. The goal is to make investments that capture profits as the trend unfolds and others recognize the true value.

One of the elements to succeeding in small-cap investing is that you need to think for yourself and make your own decisions. You are unlikely to be buying the ideas presented by the financial media. Great investors are constantly looking for emerging trends to create *new* opportunities; to produce triple-digit returns, you need to think outside of the Wall Street box and stop seeking the familiar, well-known companies. There is a popular method to how most people invest, based on their first-hand experiences with products and services. They like the taste of a Big Mac so they buy McDonald's, or they like Coke more than Pepsi, so they invest in Coca-Cola. Or they know Chipotle has long lines at lunch, so they buy shares of the burrito restaurant chain. These are fine companies, but sticking with the familiar is never going to maximize your opportunities, unless you invest in the early innings.

Spotting the Next Big Idea

To find the big ideas, you need to digest vast amounts of information and formulate a working investment thesis. For example, your beginning thesis may include several elements: A game-changing product or service, creative management, exceptional and unusual marketing, and strong financial performance. This is a thesis most people can work with. But to get there, you need to look at many companies and their numbers and markets.

One theme that emerged in 2002, and has been in play ever since, is the gold commodity, which rose from $300 to $1,000 an ounce in 2009. Not only has the price of gold moved decidedly higher, but companies involved in the exploration and development of mines and production of gold have profited handsomely, as have their shareholders. Gold has been rising steadily for years, as the U.S. dollar weakened and demand from global markets increased while supply remained constrained.

The gold commodity has risen as investors sought hard assets. But it has been the companies that are engaged in the gold industry that have produced the greatest gains for their investors. In November 2008, gold had pulled back to $700 an ounce, after reaching almost $1,000 an ounce earlier in the year. The price of gold then rallied over 30 percent by early 2009, eclipsing $1,000 an ounce. Meanwhile, the Market Vectors Gold

Miners Index (NYSE: GDX) rose over 75 percent during the corresponding time period.

When it comes to a boom in the price of commodities, it is the companies engaged in business that see profits grow and their share prices soar as commodity prices move higher. Often it is the small-cap companies that grow the fastest, and the gains for their shares far exceed a move in the price of the commodity.

Let's examine small-cap gold company Aurizon Mines (AMEX: AZK), recently added to the S&P/TSX Global Gold Index, an international benchmark that tracks the biggest and best in the industry.

The Vancouver-based mining company owns Casa Berardi, a 22-mile long property holding an estimated 1.1 million ounces of gold in Quebec. The company extracts 165,000 ounces per year from this location. Aurizon's market capitalization grew to $600 million from $11 million in just seven years by the end of 2008.

Aurizon entered a joint agreement with Lake Shore Gold in 2008, enabling a combination of mining and exploration. Currently, only 20 percent of Casa Berardi is active, and Lake Shore may be able to unlock more gold beneath the property. Fiscal 2007 was Aurizon's first profitable year, and the joint venture seems to be a win-win. The combined expertise of Aurizon and Lake Shore makes the total both innovative and creative, combining the two aspects of mining and exploration. With gold prices soaring to over $1,000 per ounce in 2009, the signs were positive for continued years of profit.

Even so, the fortunes of any extraction business are going to be tied to the underlying commodity price. This holds true for precious metals such as gold and silver, base metals including copper, and oil, and natural gas.

Oil is another good example of rising commodity prices creating big opportunities for small-cap investors. Increasing global demand for oil, coupled with supply shortages out of the Middle East, Africa, and South America, resulted in a perfect storm for the price of crude oil. While the supply-demand issue played a major role in the rising price of oil, speculators created a mania for oil in 2008 that sent the price of black gold above $147 a barrel and gas above $4 a gallon for most consumers in the United States. The recession that came about in 2008 and became widespread in the later part of the year sent the price of oil swooning to $35 a barrel, making gas affordable once again, but the near-term future for oil investments less certain, with demand falling as a result of the global slowdown and increased interested in clean energy.

A small-cap investor who recognized the oil opportunity in 2000 or 2001 would want to find a small, obscure company getting into a regionally focused refining or production program, oil sand extraction, or even exploration. Many small-cap oil stocks faired very well during the period of

2001 to 2008, an extended period of price appreciation for oil. These days the small-cap investor might want to study alternative energy, companies involved with fixing the electrical grid, developing nuclear energy, or coal liquefaction, sectors that may be increasingly of interest with the United States seeking energy independence and a cleaner environment.

If you look back at past development of successful small-cap companies (including some very big names today), you will quickly realize that the way to spot the emerging trend is not by mere speculation, but by recognizing how new trends grow. Finding the next big idea in a small cap is determined by the specific factors you decide to investigate, and a combination of these should come into play to spot the next big idea, including:

1. *Excellent leadership.* The originator of a new idea is usually a visionary with an enlightened view of the future, especially for a specific product or service. These points of view go against the trend. People like Bill Gates, Michael Dell, or Steve Jobs (using computers as the example of a large trend still underway) are entrepreneurs who all had unique perspectives on the products and services they offered. The Windows system and its user-friendly interface, Dell's customer-based response system, and Apple's simple accessibility of computer technology on all levels were all revolutionary ideas in their time. Another attribute all of these examples share in common is that *at the time they were small-cap stocks;* what's more, their potential was easily recognized at the time and not only in hindsight. Of course, not everyone with a new idea is going to succeed, which comes back to the point that the entrepreneur must be exceptional, not only in the generation of ideas, but in how the ideas will be taken onto the market.

    To find the next excellent leader, you need to examine a number of prospects in fields you think are going to grow in the future. Who has the next brilliant idea? Who is taking calculated risks? Who is a visionary and not just a manager? The person who can transform an entrepreneurial spirit into a revolutionary product and who can take the market with a new approach is most likely to succeed in the future. Finding them requires a lot of reading and comparison.

2. *An idea for the time.* It is clear looking back that ideas such as fast food, home computers, and cell phones made good use of the technology of the time. Fast food restaurants were strategically placed along a newly developed system of highways to approximate distances for refueling and meal breaks. Cell phones capitalized on the technology of the day. And home computers would have been impossible in the 1950s, when all computers were expensive, bulky, and slow. A true investment opportunity demands that the idea itself is well suited to the

emerging needs and desires of the consumer *and* based on maximizing technology.

For example, Lexar Media capitalized on the booming market for everything digital, including flash drives, digital music players, and digital cameras starting in 2002. The timing of Lexar could not have been better; management gave customers exactly what they wanted in this new technology. The company was eventually bought out by one-time competitor Micron Technology, but its growth during this early period was typical of the kind of opportunity you need to find. Just how well did Lexar tap into the macro trend to digitize media? For the period of 2001 through 2005, five short years, the company saw sales jump from $74 million to $853 million, an increase of 1,059 percent, or a compounded annual growth rate of 63.2 percent a year! Shares of Lexar fared well, soaring 444 percent from $3.49 when I alerted my readers about the company in October 2002 to $19 when the company was bought by Micron.

3. *Great growth potential*. Even the best ideas are only going to go so far if they have limited markets. If the opportunity has been fulfilled already, future growth may prove limited. The best known stock market success stories are those companies that provided goods and services with widespread appeal. But it is also companies focused on niche opportunities that are able to realize significant growth and sizable profits through unique product offerings and market dominance. Don't write off companies operating in these small markets, because the profit margins can be amazing.

Right before the price of oil started rising in 2002, Canada-listed Peyto (TSX: PEY-UN), a small but highly successful exploration and production company that later reorganized to become an energy trust, paid huge dividends while at the same time soaring in share price. While most energy trusts didn't have the ongoing concern mentality and were set up strictly as one-time entities to take advantage of immediate favorable tax implications, Peyto took the approach of sustainability originating from capital reinvestment in conjunction with regular dividend disbursements. Most other energy trusts fizzled out after heavy payouts and ran their course; Peyto did not view this to be the proper approach, nor did it consider dividends and capital reinvestment to be mutually exclusive, and as such it has been able to continue to capitalize on its favorable tax structure and, more important, to continue to reward investors. The period of 2002 through August 2005 saw the stock appreciate from $1.16 to $30.68, far eclipsing the 100 percent increase in the price of oil over the same period of time.

A good example from the previous chapter, BankRate (Nasdaq: RATE), shows what I mean by strong growth candidates. This is a story of a stock that had incredibly strong financial performance and saw its shares rise as a result. The stock flew under the radar and was overlooked by many investors for two reasons: It was an Internet stock in the post-dot-com bust, and its trading status on the OTC BB exchange, which is known for listing low-quality stocks.

A bit of history: BankRate went public in 1999 right in the midst of the infamous dot-com boom. They raised $40 million and went on a massive spending spree, and the company was ranked eighth on the *Barron's* Burn Rate List in 2000. By that time they had hired more than 200 employees, opened six subsidiaries, and were going through $2.9 million a month (with $12.8 million in the bank at the time, this gave BankRate only four months to live).

But with a new all-star leadership team and direction, BankRate managed a successful turnaround that put the company on track for profits and rewarded investors handsomely. The company closed down most of their subsidiaries, slashing 105 positions, and began focusing on their core business. Unlike so many Internet ventures in the late 1990s, they survived and thrived. By 2002, when I presented this company to my subscribers, BankRate had $8 million in cash on hand, no debt, and reported quarterly earnings of $690,000 on revenues of $5.9 million, or 11.7 percent profit margins. I saw value in the company, and I alerted my subscribers to this opportunity when the stock was trading at $1.

The superior financial results of the company demonstrated great performance, but the stock remained overlooked in 2002. By 2008, shares traded as high as $55, providing early investors who made a contrary bet on an out-of-favor industry gains of 5,500 percent!

4. *Growing exposure.* The best time to invest in a promising small cap is when it is undiscovered today, but has growing exposure. This means the company will be ignored by most analysts, but it has started to gain the attention of a limited number of institutions, and it has little or no coverage in the mainstream financial media, which tend to focus on well-known "newsworthy" companies everyone knows by name.

True Religion Apparel (Nasdaq: TRLG) has been a real success story in bucking the trend of foreign produced clothing by domestically producing denim clothing. The company got exposure by giving its high-end jeans to celebrities and gaining great press worth millions when celebs such as Alex Rodriguez, Britney Spears, and Gwyneth Paltrow were seen in pictures in the gossip rags sporting True Religion jeans. The company fulfilled growing consumer demand by selling to high-profile department stores, boutiques, and through its own store. The company manufactures premium denim wear for the fashion-conscious market in North America, Asia, and Europe. Their jeans sell for as high as $465 a pair. Men's lines include jackets, shirts, and a corduroy line; they produce women's jeans, jackets, shirts, skirts, and shorts. They also offer a children's line of clothing. About 75 percent of all sales come from specialty retail stores, as well as high-end big name retailers like Neiman Marcus, Bergdorf Goodman, and Saks Fifth Avenue. My subscribers got in early on True Religion when we bought the stock in August 2004 at just over $1 per share. Shares ultimately went as high as $31 in 2008, providing my readers with gains of as much as 3,100 percent .

In 2003, the company reported $2.4 million in sales with a net loss of $10,700. In 2004, they booked earnings of $4.2 million on sales of $27.6 million. In 2005, revenues jumped almost fourfold to $102.5 million. The company's net income for the year was $19.5 million. True Religion is another example of an outstanding small-cap stock that came public on the less well-regarded OTC BB exchange, but moved to the well-regarded Nasdaq exchange in 2005, signifying the progress and financial performance of the company in recent years.

5. *Truly "small" capitalization.* When a company has relatively few shares in the public float and total capitalization is less than $500 million, the timing is ideal and future growth is most likely. At this point, the growth cycle is just starting, and the company is quite young. Share value is most likely to appreciate rapidly, as investor interest (and demand) increases. In fact, most of the best performing stocks over a five or 10-year period have been those with market capitalizations below $100 million, indicating that even within the broad small-cap definition of less than $2 billion, smaller is definitely better if big gains are your goal.

6. *Competitive edge.* The small-cap company also must hold a real competitive edge, a distinction from its peers, and a focus on delivering what the customer wants. This can be accomplished through distribution or strategic partnerships, a new sales approach, or far superior product or service.

For example, Sonic Solutions (Nasdaq: SNIC) started out selling CD burning software, but made its big move when it expanded into DVD burning at just the right time: the beginning of the digital media trend with consumers wanting to create their own CDs and DVDs. It competed soundly by bundling software in computers sold by Dell (Nasdaq: DELL), Gateway, and Compaq, resulting in very low product cost and great profit margins. Additionally, this strategy put Sonic Solutions at a distinct advantage over its competitors, since its software was installed on the desktop of most new computers being sold by the big industry players.

7. *Managed growth trend.* One of the big dangers with rapid growth occurs when a company outpaces its own resources. Expanding too quickly

can take a great idea and dash it on the rocks of cash flow shortages, excessive expenses, or loss of direction in the market.

Look for consistency in the debt ratio and working capital ratios to spot good cash flow policies; these are explained in more detail in the financial chapter.

Expanding Your Search

Limit your research to a few key areas. Looking to the past, you can see how evolving technology often highlights where you should search. Major technological developments like the telephone, automobile, airplane, transistor, microchip, home computer, Internet, and wireless communications are only the most obvious among a big list of previous new ideas. What new ideas are emerging today? To make gains as a small-cap investor, you need to be able to identify the industry before the rest of the market also sees it.

Checking the news is a good starting point. But also talk to people and find out what they know and what interests them. The evolution of defense technology is continually ongoing, and given the current state of alert worldwide against terrorism, preventive security has become a new and emerging field of interest. This involves everything from airport security systems to surveillance devices, satellite technology, and detection devices for everything from explosives to radioactivity. These technologies were virtually unheard of only a few decades ago.

One way to spot emerging new ideas is through observing what is becoming obsolete. As one product becomes outdated, it is rapidly replaced by something that is better, faster, and cheaper. Some examples of past products falling out of favor:

- Polaroid revolutionized the camera industry by developing the instant camera. Unfortunately for the company, its growth was a one-time deal, and it was not able to keep up with ever-improving cameras with advanced lenses, auto-focus, and other innovations. The market was quickly overrun by more aggressive, emerging companies promoting faster, cheaper, and more innovative camera technology.
- Kodak grew over 100 years by dominating the film industry. But management was so committed to its film product lines that it failed to see how digital cameras were changing the world. Today, Kodak has entered the digital market quite late and is struggling to catch up with its entrepreneurial peers, which started out as small caps and grew rapidly to command the market. Companies like Sony, HP, and Xerox are far ahead, and the big question is whether or not Kodak can reinvent itself.

Looking to the future, you want to find *replacement* technologies and ideas. What is going obsolete today? And how is old or expensive technology being replaced with new, more affordable alternatives?

Disruptive technologies such as open source software versus proprietary software include companies like Redhat (NYSE: RHT) versus Novell's Suse or Open Office versus MS Office.

Another huge shift has been toward the Software as a Service (SaaS) model versus the more traditional localized software. Salesforce (NYSE: CRM) is a great example of a stock that should do well in a strong bull market, when technology tends to lead the trend. As a business model, SaaS is recession-proof because it lowered business costs, but even stocks in this sector took a beating in the crash of 2008.

Examples of industrial giants falling away due to obsolete products or obsolete management decisions make the point. Some may be able to change and catch up; most will not. The same will be true of emerging small-cap companies, especially in technology sectors, where rapid changes define success for some and failure for others. All of these examples of how historical mistakes have had consequences make the point, however. To spot emerging and new technological advances, look for what is outdated and you will find a replacement product and technology.

The Competitive Edge

The mistakes made by yesterday's giants are instructive for small-cap investors. Despite the best efforts at bringing together all of the elements that are likely to make a company grow, it is a common mistake to simply get too big and too lazy. Company management has to remain diligent to be competitive. As the saying goes, "A new chief executive officer today, exhausted by the climb to the peak, falls down on the mountaintop and goes to sleep."[1]

A small cap grows with good management, strong financial results and—most of all—a competitive edge. Having a one-of-a-kind product or a creative way of approaching the market is essential, but in order for a small cap to dominate its industry, it has to take and hold the competitive edge.

One example is a company based in Santa Paula, California. Calavo Growers (Nasdaq: CVGW) has strategic advantages in bushels. The company started in the 1920s as a California avocado growers' cooperative, eventually going public in 2001. It sources avocados from other locales, chiefly Mexico and Chile, and sells into international markets. In 2005, Calavo was the first company to market avocados in China. With a market capitalization of less than $200 million, the company is a dominant player in processed and fresh avocados. By transitioning from a growers' cooperative to a public company, Calavo took the strategic steps needed to evolve into an international agribusiness. It reduced its California weather risk by transforming itself to both major importer and exporter; today, Calavo is the largest packer of Mexican-grown avocados.

The company added breadth to its markets by purchasing Maui Fresh International, Inc. in 2003, a multi-product distributor of processed and packaged tropical fruits and chilies. Since then, Calavo has entered a distribution agreement for export of tomatoes from Mexico to the United States and another marketing deal for fresh mushrooms. Hawaiian pineapples and papayas also are coming into the mainland through Calavo.

Calavo holds many strategic advantages based on key demographics of its customers. People increasingly want to eat healthy, and avocados are growing in popularity, both fresh and processed. U.S. consumption more than doubled from 1996 to 2005 to 516,100 tons, as imports and availability increased. Calavo also has a stock purchase agreement with Limoneira (Pink Sheets: LMNR), whose holdings include 7,000 California agricultural acres offering commercial and housing development opportunities. The agreement calls for Calavo to market Limoneira's avocado crop while both companies maximize packing efficiencies by consolidating operations, a profitable venture for both companies.

Calavo's dividend by 2008 was at two percent. But even with the strong development of new markets, its stock price languished between $9 and $12 per share from 2005 to 2007. During this time, an attentive investor who monitored the company could easily see that Calavo was methodically building its niche and diversifying its business. Earnings doubled between 2005 and 2007, and revenues increased from $260 million to $303 million.

When Calavo was first featured in my small-cap newsletter in early May 2007, shares were near $12. They had doubled by October. Calavo's five-year annualized return was near 18 percent in mid-2008, compared with a seven percent gain for the S&P Packaged Foods and Meats Index. Early investors in Calavo got the prize. They bought before the all-important institutional investors who bid up the share price as they acquired significant positions.

Spotting Institutional Activity

Spotting institutional ownership is important because getting invested before these larger investors is a surefire way to big profits.

Institutional investors eventually recognized the value of Calavo, and it became a holding of many large firms. By 2009, 22 percent of the stock was owned by institutional investors. These institutional investors—mutual funds, pension funds, hedge funds, banks, and other financial institutions—manage trillions of dollars, moving in and out of investments every month, mostly well-known mid and large caps. Representing roughly two-thirds of the capitalization of the entire U.S. stock market, institutional capital drives the direction of share values. These investors must buy large positions to have a real impact on their overall portfolio, often meaning millions of dollars of buying. It doesn't take more than a couple big institutional buyers to send share prices soaring. But institutions are too big to recognize small-cap opportunities at their earliest stages, instead they want to buy proven companies with longer track records of success.

The goal of individual investors is to buy great growth companies that are performing well and are reasonably priced before the institutional investors step in and start buying a stock. This means that you want to ideally time your purchases before a company attracts widespread attention. The timing is less important than finding the right company; if you find the right company and can buy and hold the stock, the future profits will be well worth the wait—even if it takes several months or even years for institutional investors to realize the value of your great small-cap stock.

Timing the entry ahead of institutions is difficult, but worth attempting. Timing is a tricky task, but it's much like picking raw land in the path of progress. The only way to know is when some developers are starting to look themselves; you cannot merely guess at where the path is moving. Developers show initial interest in land based on traffic flow, population growth, topography, demand, and—if they are smart—how well they can control the growth itself. This is the same idea with small-cap investing. Once a company is widely owned by institutional investors, it is unlikely that the stock will recognize huge gains, unless of course the company is the next Dell or Microsoft. While attempting to find the next Dell or Microsoft can be a goal, I have demonstrated that you don't need to invest in future big-name companies to achieve stellar portfolio gains.

There are several ways to spot institutional interest. The quickest is to analyze volume: What you want to see is extraordinary volume accompanied by an upward price direction. Using three-month average volume as a benchmark, watch for a considerable increase in volume from the beginning level to 50 percent or more. If this volume uptick is accompanied by an appreciable increase in stock price, it's a sign that institutional investors are starting to move into the stock. If volume rises but the stock price doesn't, it's a sign that early investors are selling into the influx of new orders. And a drop on heavy volume is a bad omen. It usually means the big money is heading for the door. While the institutions might not be right, it doesn't matter. Ideally, you want institutional interest as one factor to drive up the price, but not too early. The best time for this to occur is at the same time that you begin buying shares.

An Example

International Assets Holding Corp. (Nasdaq: IAAC), a financial services group that focuses on select international markets, concentrates on five markets: international equities market-making, international debt capital markets, foreign exchange trading, commodities trading, and asset management.

IAAC doubled in just over two-and-a-half months, largely due to institutional interest. From June 30, 2006, to September 30, 2006, the number of institutional investors grew from seven to 17, of which 12 also added to their positions. Prices rallied from near $15 at the end of June to above $40 in early December. Daily volume in IAAC rested beneath 50,000 shares until June, when it began to climb as share prices rose. Volume eclipsed the 500,000 mark in June, and then topped out after bursting over the two-million-share threshold in December.

Understanding the implications of volume is a valuable tool. Your investment decisions should be made based on sound fundamental analysis. However, the volume trend is important as well. By accessing a range of information and understanding the implications for your investment decisions, you will beef up your profits.

The idea is to be in a stock just before large-scale institutional interest and to get out right before institutional distribution. It is difficult to pinpoint precise timing of these events, but it is possible to spot the trend. Financial websites list average and daily volume figures, and major exchanges have sections on their websites detailing institutional holdings as well as buy and sell activity.

The Bottom Line

- Small-cap companies are overlooked by Wall Street, resulting in less competition and reasonable valuations.
- A theme-based approach to investing means finding specific investment opportunities that can capitalize on big ideas.
- Recognizing how new trends grow will point you to sectors ripe for investment.
- Big winners are beneficiaries of growth trends, such as Microsoft with the home computer and Wal-Mart with the shopping super store.
- Watch for signs of institutional buying as an indicator to time your entry to small caps.
- Information is available, but it is not efficiently distributed; Finding the gems requires diligence and work, but the rewards are considerable.
- Widespread media coverage likely means the early profits have already been made.

CHAPTER 3

Finding Great Small-Cap Stocks

"Experience taught me a few things. One is to listen to your gut, no matter how good something sounds on paper. The second is that you're generally better off sticking with what you know. And the third is that sometimes your best investments are the ones you don't make."

—Donald Trump

"Only buy something that you'd be perfectly happy to hold if the market shut down for 10 years."

—Warren Buffett

Over the years, I've examined hundreds of small-cap stocks for Small-CapInvestor.com, my other investment services, and my personal investment portfolio. During that time, I've developed a focused investment style and philosophy, based on ideas and strategies that have worked time and again.

I'll put those ideas into action by showcasing Graham (AMEX: GHM), one small-cap stock I recommended on SmallCapInvestor.com. This company is a great example of the investment potential you can find in many small-cap stocks. I'll show you exactly how I evaluated this company, so you can take those lessons and apply the approach to your own investments in the future.

Growth + Value = Profits

I simply don't believe the terms "value" and "growth" are mutually exclusive. A stock can be undervalued and at the same time outperform as a growth stock. In flat or down markets, it's always sensible to search for companies whose true value has not yet been recognized. And, if the markets begin to move, what better candidates for extraordinary growth than those same undervalued stocks?

Many investors consider themselves to be either "growth investors" or "value investors."

Growth investors typically buy companies that are expanding quickly and that are categorized as being in growth industries (those that are experiencing more rapid growth than the economy as a whole). They are more concerned with the opportunity for the future profitability than they are in the operating history and performance.

Value investors tend to focus on buying stocks that are bargains— typically due to poor financial performance, an out-of-favor sector, short-term mismanagement, or slow growth. These investors aim to buy stocks at a discount, with the idea that performance will improve and the stock prices will rise over the long-term.

My system for finding great small-cap stocks combines both a growth and value approach, taking the best of both worlds and applying these principles to understanding the prospects of the company while weighing this into every investment decision. Fundamentally, I am a growth investor, seeking to buy stocks at a reasonable price with maximum appreciation potential.

This philosophy is also based on finding companies that are undervalued by the market. Whether it's a question of overreaction to a certain bit of bad news or some other development, the company's stock price—in the eyes of value investors—simply doesn't reflect the value of the company itself. By early 2009, for example, the market was in an unusual position: There were more undervalued stocks than those fairly valued due to the pessimism and fear dominating the market at that time.

While value investing focuses on a company's intrinsic value, growth investing is meant to find stocks with the potential for earnings and revenue growth and financial outperformance. If you look at it another way, value investing emphasizes what already exists, and growth investing looks to the future.

How I balance these two depends on the movement of the overall market and on action in the individual stock. As markets run, high-growth, momentum stocks outpacing the market command a price premium. On the flip side, in a down market, as growth expectations are reduced, valuations contract and most stocks move lower. While bear markets can give the illusion of undervalued stocks, it is important to keep in mind the fact that valuations have contracted due to a perceived slowdown in future growth or poor financial performance. Investors must not buy everything when the market declines. Rather, it is important to find those solid companies with strong prospects that are oversold, undervalued, and poised to recover before the broader market. More often than not, it is the innovative growth companies we know of as small caps that recover first.

Finding great investments, based on growth and value, requires a few basic and logical steps. The first step is often overlooked: Get to know the company behind the stock as thoroughly as possible. Remember, when you buy a stock you're buying a piece of a company, you're becoming an owner. In the same manner you wouldn't buy a home sight unseen, you shouldn't buy a stock without performing your due diligence. I'm amazed at how many people will buy a stock without having at least a working knowledge of the company. Investors need to know what a company does. What products does it sell? What is the background of the management team? How has the company performed financially? And, what are the prospects for the future?

Buying a stock without being able to answer these basic questions is a mistake. It's like going to a doctor to perform surgery without asking about qualifications, training, or rates of successful treatment. The same holds true for choosing winning small-cap stocks; if you don't know the company, all the numbers and metrics won't make much sense.

Spotting the Right Company

How do you find out about a company? Get a prospectus (it outlines the company's activities, financials, and other details) and its most recent annual and quarterly reports; these can usually be viewed or downloaded on a company's website. Do a Google search on the company and ticker symbol. See if it's been mentioned in the media (but remember that a magazine cover story doesn't make it a good investment). If you have friends or colleagues who invest, see if the company has come to their attention. If the company is nearby, pay a visit to get a first-hand look or call the investor relations department of the company and ask some tough questions (these investor relations professionals love talking with prospective investors and should be a resource for gathering information; keep in mind, though, they are trying to get you to buy their stock, so they are biased).

Investment newsletters and financial web sites such as my SmallCapInvestor.com also help in the discovery process. In February 2008, I alerted my subscribers to Graham Corp. (AMEX:GHM), a company in Batavia, New York. My research report on the company answered the following basic questions:

- *What does the company do?* Graham designs and builds custom vacuum and heat transfer equipment for heavy industrial customers. Graham's products include steam jet ejector vacuum systems, surface condensers for steam turbines, vacuum pumps, compressors, and heat exchangers.
- *Who are the customers?* Graham's products are used in a number of industrial processes in a variety of industries, including oil refining, chemicals, pharmaceuticals, plastics, fertilizers, liquefied natural gas production, soap manufacturing, and air conditioning systems manufacturing.

Graham's systems are also used in alternative power generating facilities, such as nuclear, cogeneration, and geothermal plants.

- *Is the industry growing?* Despite some softening in the United States during 2008, strong growth in Brazil, Russia, India, and China caused a global wave of investment in the petrochemical, oil refining, and electric power generation industries. Feedstocks were also having an impact on equipment demand; existing petrochemical plants adapted to sour crude as sweet crude reserves were depleted. Demand also spiked due to Middle East natural gas plant construction, increased geothermal demand in various regions, and the worldwide shortage of oil refining capacity.
- *What's the latest news from the company?* Graham announced in 2008 a $1.8 million order for surface condensers to be installed in a coal-to-liquid facility in China. Coal-to-liquid is an emerging technology used to liquefy coal and upgrade output into petroleum-based products, in this case methanol, which is then converted into ethylene.
- *What is the future?* Graham's CEO, Jim Lines, focuses a lot of attention on the emerging energy sector as coal-to-liquid, gas-to-liquid, and bio-diesel became industry buzzwords. This is becoming the energy sector's new emphasis.

The more you know about a company—where it's been and where it might be headed—the more informed your investing decision will be. And, just as important, all that knowledge places the next step in the process into clearer context: the numbers behind the company.

Due diligence doesn't stop when you decide to buy a stock. It is equally important to understand *why* a company's stock fared well or not after your purchase. This will help you make decisions about when to sell the stock, and it will help you make future purchasing decisions.

Why did the stock perform in the manner it did? In Graham's case, the stock ran from a price of $17.30 on February 21, 2008 (the date I recommended Graham as a stock to buy) to $43.91 on July 14, 2008, for a gain of 154 percent. From its peak, Graham fell to a price of $10 on January 22, 2009. This coincided with oil's run; U.S. Oil Fund (USO), the exchange-traded fund used as a proxy for oil, showed similar movement, from a price of $77.33 to $117.48 during 2008, a gain 51.9 percent, before falling to $30.02 on January 22, 2009. The takeaway here is that Graham, by the very business it's engaged in, benefits from higher oil prices as Figure 3.1 shows.

The Oil Boom and Bust of 2008

Graham was only a part of the bigger oil and gas industry picture. Sweeping trends, by definition, don't happen overnight. Consider the summer of 2008,

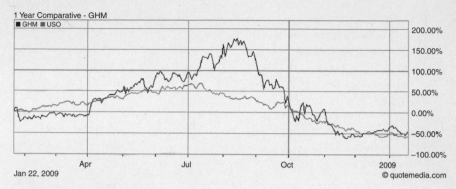

FIGURE 3.1 Graham Corp.

Source: QuoteMedia

when gasoline prices surged well past $4 per gallon for the first time. It happened very quickly, but the fact is those exploding prices had been in the works for years. Have a look at this timeline:

- The United States invaded Iraq in 2003. Iraq has the world's third largest proven petroleum reserves and some of the lowest extraction costs, according to the U.S. Energy Information Administration. But just a fraction of its known fields are in development, hindered—as is Iraq's output and exports—by continued hostilities. Iraq produced about 2.5 million barrels of oil per day in early 2002, but that fell to 2 million barrels by 2008. Exports fell from a 2004 high of 2.5 million to 1.5 million in 2006. Light crude futures on the New York Mercantile Exchange were $40 per barrel.
- Hurricane Katrina disrupted supplies from the Gulf, causing a spike in 2005. Light crude hit $80 a barrel.
- In 2007, prices climbed as U.S. stockpiles fell. Light crude approached the $100 mark.
- The $100 per barrel mark was breached in 2008, exacerbated by news of falling production in key suppliers such as Venezuela.
- Light crude jumped to $147 by the middle of 2008 in a speculation driven mania for the commodity, instigated by high demand from emerging markets and the U.S., coupled with lower production.

Figure 3.2 illustrates the price movement of oil during the period, although a slowing worldwide economy dropped the price per barrel to below $30 by the end of 2008.

Given the volatility of oil prices in recent years, the roadmap pointing to energy-related investments—not to mention alternative energy source–related investments—was on the drawing board for years. This applies to

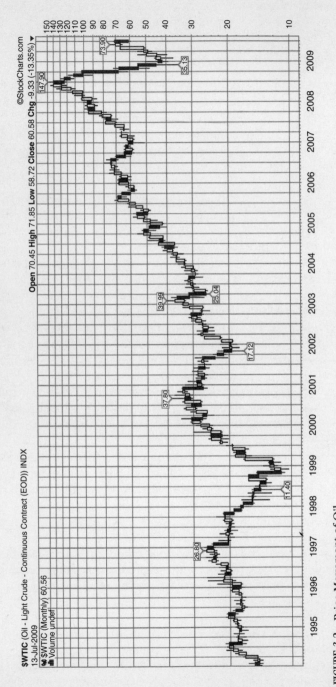

FIGURE 3.2 Price Movement of Oil

Source: Chart courtesy of StockCharts.com

other areas as well. A lot of technology evolves over years or even decades. So entry into a new or emerging market has to be timed carefully.

Putting It All Together—The Graham Example

Picking winning small-cap stocks isn't for investors looking for mindless slam dunks. Rather, the process is involved and challenging, but for investors willing to do the work, the rewards can be significant.

To help pull the elements together, let's take a look at the numbers for Graham Corporation at the time my SmallCapInvestor.com first recommended a buy in 2008:

- *Revenue:* Revenue for the third fiscal quarter 2008 was $20.6 million, up 42 percent from $14.5 million in the same period one year before.
- *Net income:* Net income was up from $666,000 the year before to $3.8 million in the third fiscal quarter 2008.
- *Diluted earnings per share:* Diluted EPS was $0.74 in the third fiscal quarter 2008 versus $0.14 in the same quarter the year before.
- *Gross profit:* 41.9 percent of sales in the third fiscal quarter 2008 versus 23.4 percent in the year before. The company cited improved operating efficiency and outsourcing for the year-over-year gains.
- *Sales:* For the first nine months of fiscal 2008, sales were $63.7 million, up 41 percent from $45 million for the first nine months of fiscal 2007.
- *Cash balance:* At December 31, 2007, the company had $33 million in cash, cash equivalents, and short-term investments, more than double its position ($15.1 million) as of March 31, 2007, only nine months before.
- *Analyst estimates of earnings per share:* $2.31 in fiscal year 2008 and $2.52 in 2009 on revenues of $83.5 million and $93 million, respectively.
- *P/E:* At the time of the recommendation, based on estimates, Graham's price-earnings ratio was around 15.
- *Market capitalization:* $169 million.

This is just a sampling of the factors taken into consideration in recommending Graham. The company was consistent in many of the principles I use for picking small-cap stocks, namely a strong earnings trend, growth in cash on hand, positive analysts' estimates, and an attractive price-earnings ratio.

Top-performing stocks in a sector tied to a commodity such as oil will outperform the growth of the underlying commodity experiencing a bull run. For example, shares of Graham outperformed the move in the price of oil by a factor of 3-to-1. For this reason, it is important for small-cap investors to focus on identifying the big trends, and then finding those select small-cap companies with exposure to the growth opportunities that are likely to capture big profits. This example highlights the rewards that are bestowed upon those investors who can identify trends and find great companies within a sector that have an ability to perform and excel.

Thus, when I formally recommended Graham, the shares were trading at a split-adjusted $17.30 per share. By August 2008, the stock price advanced to $53.34 a share. Yet, by the end of the year, the price had fallen to just under $11 per share, a symptom of the market-wide decline in stock values. However, my newsletter had sold out of Graham on July 25 at $38.99 per share, a gain of 125 percent in only five months.

This raises another important cautionary point about all types of investing: A market-wide decline affects all stocks, even the great value and growth stocks, if only temporarily. It is often wise to protect paper profits with stop-loss orders and diversification (more on these ideas later in the book).

Not every small-cap stock has the growth potential that Graham exhibited within the time frame of a year—that's why you need to do your homework. But this does demonstrate that, with the proper discipline, exhaustive attention to important details, and a willingness to go the extra distance, you can find small-cap stocks with superior growth prospects. It is these stocks that are likely to provide the biggest gains.

Success Stories from the Past

Every well-known mid-cap and large-cap company started out as a small cap. Some notable successes of the past make the point that successful companies have gone through years of amazing growth in many cases. One such company is Dell.

Michael Dell started this company in his college dorm room with about $1,000 in personal savings. The value of Dell stock exploded by more than 36,000 percent at its peak; that initial $1,000 investment has grown into the greatest stock market success of all time, with Dell sporting market capitalization of more than $21 billion at the beginning of 2009 (see Figure 3.3).

Large companies like Dell aren't the only big companies that started small. There are many like Dell, selling products or services to you and your network of family, friends, and colleagues. Many companies with a great product or service are potential investments.

For example, if you boat, hunt, hike, or fish, you're probably aware of the value of a solid global positioning system. And, chances are good you've heard of Garmin (Nasdaq: GRMN), a producer of GPS receivers for the marine and outdoor recreation markets.

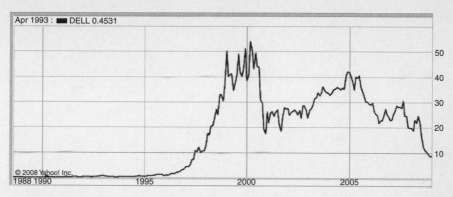

FIGURE 3.3 Dell Shares Soar: 1988 to 2008
Source: Yahoo! Inc.

By 1995, Garmin's sales had reached $105 million and turned a healthy profit of $23 million. By 1999, sales reached $233 million and profits soared to $64 million. That same year, the company's products captured roughly half of the North American market share for GPS receivers used in the marine and outdoor recreation markets, according to a study by Frost and Sullivan.[1] By 2000, Garmin had sold three million GPS devices and was producing 50 different models. Its products were sold in 100 countries and carried by 2,500 independent distributors.

Translation: If you enjoy the outdoors, you probably were aware of Garmin. And, since Garmin's products were so popular, that meant consumers valued them for their quality and reliability. In fact, you might well have owned and used one yourself based on those very same attributes.

Now, let's take a look at the performance of Garmin stock during the period of 2000 through 2007. Shares of Garmin began trading on the NASDAQ stock exchange on December 8, 2000, when the company's IPO was introduced. Shares were priced at $14, and closed the day at $20.12. During the following years, Garmin's financial performance made the company a top performer, and gave early shareholders impressive returns. The company's stock hit a high of $121.14 on September 27, 2007, an increase of 765 percent from the IPO price seven years earlier.

As an investor, you must be aware of the products and services that you and others use. Think about what you're doing right now. Of course, you're reading this book. Are you using an electronic reader? Who manufactured the device? Who made the components? What are you sitting on? Are you at home or traveling somewhere? What clothes are you wearing? If you're hungry or thirsty, what products come to mind? And, if there are others around you, what are they doing and wearing? What do your friends, business associates, children, and others in your life use and enjoy?

Dell Inc. Personalizes the Personal Computer

A compelling angle to Dell's meteoric rise is not so much what the company sells—you can buy a personal computer from any number of companies—but how it chose to sell them. Rather than using a network of stores to distribute its products, Dell was the first PC manufacturer to pioneer direct-to-consumer sales. Dell forged a one-on-one relationship with its customers, allowing lower prices by cutting out the reseller and delivering easily customized computers to meet customers' individual needs.

How would you, as an investor, have been clued into Michael Dell's epiphany that consumers were tired of plodding to the store, dealing with commission-hungry salespeople and settling for a computer that wasn't precisely what they wanted at a price that was likely more than they wanted to pay? By tuning your crystal ball into the same frequency as Dell's? By being lucky enough to be Michael's college roommate, picking your way around wires and hard drives?

Not at all. You just had to pay attention.

It would be virtually impossible to know just what was going on in some college kid's Austin, Texas, dorm room. But the idea behind Dell isn't nearly as inaccessible. Take a minute to think about your own shopping and buying habits. Do you enjoy dealing with salespeople who may or may not know the product they're hawking? Do you like settling for something that's less than you want or need? Do you enjoy the convenience and expediency of shopping from home and buying precisely what you like without unnecessary add-ons and features?

Your answers, in order, no doubt are:

No.

Are you kidding?

Of course I do.

And so do millions of other consumers, as Dell's success amply demonstrates. And, to answer the question of how you would have found a stock such as Dell, since you knew what you liked and disliked about shopping for a computer, all you had to do was watch for a company that addressed those likes and dislikes.

No great company—and, as a point of connection, its stock—operates in a vacuum. No idea exists wholly autonomously. Rather, great companies are based on ideas that respond to a need, identify an opportunity, or offer a fresh perspective. Put another way, great companies (and great small-cap stock opportunities) don't simply happen; they happen for a reason. For example, if you have a home computer, you have undoubtedly heard of Dell. This applies to other situations, too.

IPOs Are the Genesis of Small Caps

Some of the best performing IPOs in the late 1990s included Internet startups that soon became household names like Dell and Garmin. We all know small companies that have grown to become mainstream successes. Think about it: Have you ever bought or sold anything on eBay?

eBay (Nasdaq: EBAY) is the world-famous online auction concern. It's almost impossible to imagine that you don't know someone who has bought or sold on eBay. Since its founding in 1995, eBay has grown into the preeminent online auction site worldwide, with 86 million users at the end of 2008 and $60 billion in goods and services changing hands. eBay came public in 1998 with a market capitalization of $715 million.

That kind of notoriety and dominance in a fresh playing field—person-to-person e-commerce—has translated to strong stock performance. When the company's initial public offering hit the market in September 1998, shares bolted to a one-day price jump of $43.78—nearly triple the original price. eBay shares eventually rose to a high of nearly $60 in late 2004. Anyone who has garage sale leftovers will probably end up putting them on eBay. Or if you want to buy virtually anything from antiques to books, eBay is one place you'll likely look.

Another source for books (and more) brings me to a different success story: Amazon.com (Nasdaq: AMZN). This merchant has transformed online retailing, taking in not merely books but electronics, home goods, sporting equipment, and even organic food. But the model was more than just virtual shelf after virtual shelf of goods—Amazon tracked consumer likes and dislikes, offered shopping suggestions, and effectively built a one-to-one customer relationship unlike anything on the Internet.

That model has driven solid stock performance. Despite concerns about initial public offerings from technology companies, Amazon's stock jumped from $18 to $23.50 on the day it began trading in May 1997 (the price had gone as high as $30 in intra day trading, before sliding back). By the end of 1998, adjusting for stock splits, Amazon stock had topped $350. Amazon, too, came public as a small cap with a market capitalization of $503 million. It has been an online success story among many others. Even after the dot-com crash and bear market of 2008, Amazon still was trading at $80 per share, well ahead of the IPO price.

However, online companies are not the only examples. You might buy a computer online through Dell, or you might prefer to go into a store and talk to a salesperson. In that case, you'll eventually end up in Best Buy (NYSE: BBY). This retailer started as an electronics store in St. Paul, Minnesota. Best Buy was not the only electronics retailer to push the concept of a superstore with scads of electronic goodies available under one roof. But Best Buy took the idea a step further by realizing that many consumers walking into such a techno-Xanadu were ready to find the item they wanted rather than having to endure the badgering of salespeople.

So Best Buy shifted its focus. Its stores featured well-stocked showrooms averaging 36,000 square feet, fewer salespeople, more self-help product information, answer centers for those who needed assistance, and one-stop purchasing. The company later augmented brick and mortar locations with bestbuy.com, an online service that offered direct home delivery or quick in-store pickup. And though there have been bumps along the way, a stock that debuted at $13.50 in 1985 with a market capitalization of $112 million has gone as high as $106 (adjusted for stock splits).

Translate these three stories to your own experience. If you've shopped at eBay, Amazon, or Best Buy, what stands out? Were you impressed by the service, pricing, or customer support? Was there anything that might have made you think: "This is a well-run operation. I wonder if their stock reflects the great experience that I just had?"

Take that awareness in another direction. For example, if you're traveling on a plane, did you take off on time? How's the service, the enthusiasm—or lack of enthusiasm—of the crew? How was the food (if, in fact, there is any, short of bonsai-sized bags of pretzels that would starve a single-cell organism)? If you're sitting next to someone, ask them if they fly this airline often. Are they satisfied? Do they fly it because it's more reliable or less expensive than its competitors?

Most airlines haven't exactly been world beaters as far as investment returns are concerned. But one I noticed in 2008 was Hawaiian Holdings (Nasdaq: HA), operator of Hawaiian Airlines. A terrific small cap, the value of its stock jumped 175 percent within a year, thanks to a viable and sustainable business model—attributes that you might pick up on through the overall quality of its service or the satisfaction of its passengers. American Airlines, United Airlines, or US Airways could learn something from this company! As consumers increasingly complain about poor service, in 2007 Hawaiian Airlines earned top marks in the annual airline quality survey conducted by the University of Nebraska at Omaha Aviation Institute, named number one among all carriers surveyed in on-time reliability. If you know the frustration of dealing with airline delays and cancellations, it's no wonder that Hawaiian Holdings' stock has blossomed, given its record of success.

Think about your shopping habits, too. Whether you're flying or buying a TV, the same rule applies. While TV shopping and during the course of chatting with a salesperson, maybe he reminded you of the government-mandated elimination of standard broadcast definition format in 2009. Not only would—and did—that make piles of televisions obsolete, it also produced an intrinsic demand for the technology behind the changeover. All of which at the time suggested great potential for a chip manufacturer like Techwell Inc. (NASDAQ: TWLL), whose semiconductors enabled the conversion of analog video signals to digital form.

While your first thought may have been of the government-mandated digital broadcasting transition, Techwell is so much more. This fabless (a fact I love along efficiency lines) semiconductor maker does what great companies do: profits from its core technology in multiple markets. You can find Techwell's chips in security surveillance, automotive, consumer, and personal computer markets. It's great when you find a firm operating in a fast-growing market. When I first came across Techwell, this company was operating in not just one but *four* distinct blazing markets. In mid-August 2007, Techwell was trading at $9 a share; it peaked the following June at $13.80, for a gain of more than 50 percent.

As you evaluate a company, always take some time to familiarize yourself with the market it operates in. Remember, growth has a way of hiding mistakes, and however good a firm is, it's bound to make strategic errors at some point.

You get the idea. Just by building an investor's mindset—one always open to bits of information and hints that can speak volumes about a company and potential investment for your portfolio—you can be clued in to countless investment opportunities. If you notice something that sells well or has genuine value, those attributes tend to translate to a company whose stock may be of interest to you—ideally, a small-cap stock with lots of promise.

Spotting Growth Sector Trends

Spotting big growth trends is one of the keys to successfully identifying sectors that are likely to be growing for the long-term. And it is within these growth sectors that you are likely to discover small-cap stocks that are already showing signs of rapid expansion.

Where to Look for Trends

Your goal in spotting growth sector trends is to figure out what is popular or has growing popularity.

Here are some places that you should look to identify growth trends:

- Look at products or services that you buy and love.
- Watch television news, programs, and even commercials.
- Read print media, including magazines and newspapers, and check out the cover stories.
- Talk with teenagers and people in their 20s, who often know what is hot and what is not.

A nose for news will accentuate the positive sectors and eliminate the negative. By reading the news, you know what's turning the economy's crank. You know what's driving the global trends and, in reverse, can see what sectors are spinning wheels. Your next challenge is picking an industry that is at peak performance.

Identifying the industries of champions will take you a long way toward small-cap investment success. Indeed, this step is critical: No matter how profitable or well-managed, a company will struggle to deliver gains if it is in an out-of-favor sector. Finding a stock ripe for gains in a lagging industry is like hiking the Alps: It's all uphill. You want to invest in industries with the strength to lift all companies within it.

By being a glutton for news, your sector search is much easier. You slice your investment universe of some 7,000-plus public companies down significantly. By 2008, your bank of information would have told you to stay away from the financial sector, and in fact from any organization with a whisper of exposure to the subprime debacle. Out went real estate investments, including homebuilders, Real Estate Investment Trusts, property developers, and the like.

Ditched, too, were sectors dependent on the loose change of consumers, including manufacturers, wholesalers, and retailers of apparel, electronics, toys, products for home improvement, and more. Hotels were out as vacation dollars took a holiday. Technology went on the blink as companies and consumers delayed decisions to upgrade systems, whether a call to the information technology folks or a purchase of a new personal computer. Based on daily news consumption, the kingpins of industry in the late 2000s were obvious: Commodities, including gold, oil, base metals, and even agriculture. Commodities finally got their due respect. Cries of "beans in the teens," considered an outrageous mantra for decades about soybean prices on the floor of the Chicago Board of Trade, were finally realized in 2007. Corn, wheat, eggs, meat—the stuff of a good farmer's breakfast—all soared in price, taking those companies involved in producing, servicing, and selling farm goods along for the ride.

There were magnificent gains in irrigation companies, farm equipment manufacturers and retailers, and of course, fertilizer and seed companies as farmers geared up to try to feed people, animals, and the biofuel industry. As emerging countries continued to grow in population and Gross Domestic Product (GDP), diets in these countries started to include more meat. With this expansion expected to continue, agriculture seemed like a strong industry in which to invest.

So did energy, particularly petroleum and natural gas companies, and coal. Alternative energy companies also had to be considered—wind and solar—despite a lack of government backing, which would encourage investment to develop these alternate sources. Global dynamics were just as strong if not stronger than the forces behind agriculture: Rising standards of living in emerging markets would stress energy resources as well food production.

A number of energy-related companies also responded to the record high gas and oil prices: exploration outfits, maintenance and servicing firms, drillers, and equipment manufacturers and sellers. Indeed, both agriculture and energy were experiencing what seemed a long-overdue response to global developments that could continue to move the industries to a higher price ground in coming years.

Interest in energy markets had another incentive: The volatility of the sector, which goes hand in hand with geopolitical maneuverings. The major players—OPEC countries, the Middle East region, the United States, Venezuela, and Nigeria—all have a strong sense of theater, mostly tragedy. The dynamics within the oil industry are well-entrenched and will continue to cause untoward moves in small-cap companies doing business in this tense environment.

For example, in early June 2008, crude oil prices surged to new highs near $150 per barrel after an Israeli official said an attack on Iranian nuclear facilities was inevitable because of the tight supply background. Prices were up nearly $11 from the previous day and up from less than $80 just one year earlier.

The energy sector doesn't picnic on volatility, it gorges. And, despite the mid-2008 U.S. government's calls to end a ban on offshore drilling, the end of this ban would not soon ease the supply crisis. Alternative energy, including efforts to produce clean coal, would not alleviate the tight and volatile situation either—even if Congress were to get behind energy options outside of petroleum.

For all of these reasons, this industry illustrates the next step in determining the sector in which to invest. You need two favored resources: a search of Google news for "record earnings" and www.prophet.net, which provides a nifty industry group performance listing for various time frames—from two days to up to five years.

The record earnings search shows those companies that have reported profitable milestones each day. (If you are looking for early-stage companies in a certain sector, check "record revenues" to see what trends are developing in not-yet-profitable enterprises.) Pay particular attention during quarterly earnings season, when companies' earnings come in bunches and can show exceptional power even within a strong sector.

Since your goal is to own stocks in strong sectors, run through the record earnings search looking for the industries that have a preponderance of these companies. That gives you a sense of the sector's power and shows you that the companies within it are keeping pace with the industry.

You want to own the stocks responding to sector strength and earnings growth, whose share values are accelerating as quickly as their profits. Since sector strength is so important, don't consider investing in a company in an underperforming sector even if it reports record earnings.

During the volatile year of 2008, for example, there were producers, explorers, oil servicers, and other gas and petroleum companies that drilled offshore and on land, or provided sundry products and services. They were small-caps. They were making money at an accelerating pace and—perhaps most important—their stock prices were rising just as fast, responding to both the sector strength and profit performance.

The record earnings search showed that the oil industry was a prime spot for investing. Focus on Prophet.net's three-month rankings; this time frame shows follow-through, usually incorporating two quarterly earnings periods. Viewing trends over longer periods—say, six months or a year—may not allow you to catch industrial-strength moves early, but will give a broader picture of the time frame in which a certain sector's trend has developed, cluing you in on how much power the trend is still packing.

A snapshot of this site in mid-June 2008 showed that energy-related companies were ranked high on the list of peak performers. One tool, a color-coded "industry groups performance grid," is great for exhibiting trends. For a one-year period, the strongest group was nonmetallic mineral mining, followed by agricultural chemicals. Independent oil and gas companies showed up at number seven, followed by oil and gas equipment and services at number eight. At the bottom were credit services, sporting goods, mortgage investment, title insurance, and toy stores.

The oil sector was up 26.5 percent in the three-month period. Within the industry, this sector was only outdone by oil and gas drilling and exploration companies, which were up 32.4 percent in the three-month time frame.

Those are some of the trends that have already made money for small-cap investors. The key is to look for new trends and uncover the companies that stand to benefit the most.

One way to do this is to look for trends in your own life—products you're buying, for instance, or lifestyle changes—and then seek the companies driving or pioneering these developments. Learn to identify these trends early and seek out the small, unknown high-growth companies likely to post impressive financial gains as these long-term trends unfold (and as other investors catch wind of these opportunities).

The key to success is understanding growth trends, understanding how to identify the right time to invest, and picking those true winners, while tuning out the hype and avoiding chasing trends that are past their prime. If you're reading about it on the cover of *Fortune* or *Forbes*, it is already too late.

After the 2008 Olympics in Beijing, much of the focus was on the athletes and the outcome of competitions. But another element of that coverage addressed the changing face of Chinese society and its economy.

It's no secret that the economies of emerging countries such as China have been growing faster than that of the United States. China, for instance, had a real GDP annual growth rate of 9.9 percent since free market initiatives took hold in the late 1970s (in 2007, it raced to 11.4 percent), dwarfing the snail's pace GDP growth in the United States of 3.1 percent during the same period. GDP measures the total market value of goods and services produced within a country in one year. The higher the number, the more robust the growth rate of that country's economy.

China also has 1.3 billion people, and population experts say at least one million are added to that number each month, an annual rate double the population of the state of Indiana. The middle class in China is roughly equivalent to the entire current U.S. population, 300 million. The Census Bureau estimates that the population of the United States grew at less than one percent in 2008 and will continue that slow growth rate in the future.

China's population is also changing; it's gotten younger over the years, but life expectancy also has increased. And, although most Chinese people still live in rural areas, more and more are moving to cities in search of work created by growing industrialization. This has created a huge urban demographic of concentrated demand that stresses human and natural resources, financial institutions, agriculture, and industry, as well as the country's whole system of transportation. The rapid growth in China has created a significant middle class population, with buying power for everything from condos to cars to jewelry, luxury items only affordable to the wealthy few in the past.

Even tragic events have created investment opportunities. The earthquake that socked China in early 2008 launched already-high dry bulk shipping rates even higher. That was a windfall for shipping services in the region over the short term.

Several examples of companies that benefited are Paragon Shipping (Nasdaq: PRGN), a Greek dry bulk shipper; DryShips (Nasdaq: DRYS); Diana Shipping (NYSE: DSX); and Excel Maritime Carriers (NYSE: EXM).

News You Can Use

There's a lot of news out there—both good and bad—that can point to profitable investment opportunities. This process can also be implemented from the other end of the formula—looking out for smaller companies that offer interesting ideas or products, are addressing new markets, or bringing a fresh perspective to an old issue or problem. If you read or hear about such a company, build questions based on what you know: Would I benefit from what this company has to offer? What about this company—its approach, its services—is different from what I've heard of before? To paraphrase the old Star Trek cliché, are they going where no one has gone before?

Recall the Dell example. You read about this little company in Texas that lets you buy directly from them.

Reaction: No more hand-to-hand combat with the crowds at the mall; no salespeople; tailored product design.

Reaction: No more dealing with people hired a week before who don't know RAM from ramen! You can build your computer and save money to boot.

Reaction: How can I order my computer today? And, perhaps even more important, how can I find out more about this company?

The bottom line: Being a successful small-cap investor starts with keeping your eyes and ears open for all sorts of information from all sorts of sources. What you hear, see, read, and experience tells you where you should invest as well as where you should not. You don't need to be a world-class economist; rather, the more world-class your attention level, the better your investment results will be.

You've Found an Interesting Trend or Company—Now What?

In some ways, much of the toughest work is behind you. You've come across a new trend that warrants further investigation. Or perhaps—even better—you've noticed a news item about a small company that's heavily involved in a promising trend or industry and is poised for significant growth.

Relax, it's not time yet to grab your computer mouse or the telephone to place an order for the company's stock. Paying attention enough to pick up on news or a company that's advantageously positioned to take advantage of a situation or ongoing development is only a part of the overall process.

Now it's time to take the next step and do some legwork to find out more about the company. This is not the detailed company research needed to make an investment decision. Instead, this is an intermediate exercise that will provide you with enormous insight and information. You want to learn more about something that's piqued your interest as an investor, so that you can determine whether your eye for news and information will translate into a profitable investment.

I use a number of news, information, and analytic sources at SmallCap-Investor.com to perform initial research, and, from there, I do more extensive research if the preliminary findings warrant it. Visit the websites below (most are free of charge). As you look at the features I describe, wander around the site to become comfortable and familiar with what's available.

Chances are good you'll be using them extensively in the not-too-distant future.

- *SmallCapInvestor.com* (www.SmallCapInvestor.com): In addition to information and analysis specific to small-cap stock selection, my site provides broad market commentary; analysis of news, industries, and trends; and other features that let you get a handle on information and ideas. It's also an ideal research source, both to follow up on news you hear elsewhere as well as investing ideas that our research team has generated. The format is geared to small-cap investing, so there's never any need to make the connection between news and small-cap opportunities—it's all there for you.
- *Yahoo! Finance* (finance.yahoo.com): This site offers news, analysis, and information for the small-cap investor. You can get a feel for market sentiment, which is critical if you're tracking particular news or a stock, as well as news from stock analysts, filings, and other data. Yahoo! Finance also has message boards, handy for soliciting feedback from other investors. (Caution: As with much on the Internet, take what you hear from others on message boards with a very large dose of salt. Because the Internet is a faceless medium, you can never be fully sure of the motivation or integrity of the person at the other end of the conversation. If you read something of interest, always corroborate it with another source.)
- *Investor's Business Daily* (www.investors.com): Another source of news, market trends, and investment analysis, IBD offers a "Stocks on the Move" feature, a highlighted box on the home page that focuses on stocks moving quickly up or down—and, just as important, the news or developments driving that movement. The website also devotes a substantial amount of attention to emerging trends, news, and analysis, which is valuable for following up on information you think is important in determining a small-cap investment opportunity.
- *The Wall Street Journal* (www.wsj.com): Not only does WSJ provide extensive news coverage and analysis in a timely manner, it also offers broad-based stock market commentary and ongoing focus on significant marketplace news and developments.
- *The Economist* (www.economist.com): This weekly "alternative" news source (as it labels itself) is a terrific destination for news and analysis that other media may overlook. On top of stock tracking and information, *The Economist* earmarks significant space to breaking down macroeconomic trends (economics that look at national or regional economies as a whole rather than more limited or topic-specific units). *The Economist* is a top destination for small-cap investors with ideas and

companies with investment potential, offering the extra data needed to move that potential forward.

- *Reuters* (www.reuters.com): This is another news source, but one with a greater international focus than other domestically focused sites. This is also a great site for information on institutional sponsorship, trends in institutional trading of stocks, and why.
- *Nasdaq* (www.nasdaq.com): This is the website for the National Association of Securities Dealers Automated Quotations system, the largest electronic trading venue in the world. You will find a veritable treasure trove of news, stock breakdowns, analytic tools, and other resources and information. Particularly inviting is the heavy representation of small-cap stocks among the extensive Nasdaq listings, making this site an ideal place to research small-cap companies.
- *Prophet.net* (www.prophet.net): A prime destination for investors interested in technical analysis of stocks. This information will become very useful as you grow into a successful small-cap investor.
- *EDGAR* (http://www.sec.gov/edgar.shtml): Acronym for Electronic Data Gathering, Analysis, and Retrieval, EDGAR serves as the site for comprehensive financial filings that most companies are required to make with the Securities and Exchange Commission. It reports news about quarterly and annual earnings statements, changes in leadership and ownership, and shareholder information, and it is both vast and in–depth. Given EDGAR's vast store of information that drives stock movement, this site should be on your "must visit" list.
- *Stockcharts.com* (www.stockcharts.com): This website allows you to perform comprehensive technical stock analysis, including long-term historic trends and patterns. The site also has a handy "chart school," an online tutorial that walks you through the mechanics of technical analysis.
- *Russell Investments* (www.russell.com): The Russell 2000 Index measures the performance of the 2,000 smallest companies in the Russell 3000 Index (made up of the 3,000 largest U.S. public companies). The Russell 2000 serves as a benchmark of small-cap stocks in the United States. On this website you can track the small-cap index in real time and monitor the day's winners and losers.

There are many more websites that are helpful as you investigate a small-cap company. These are some of my favorites, ones used frequently at SmallCapinvestor.com for my own research.

Like analyzing a small-cap stock itself, you simply can't be too diligent when following up on your ideas. That means rarely relying on any single source. As you find information that piques your curiosity, cross-reference it to another source. The greater the scope and balance of your initial research, the more likely you can transform that information into investment ideas with genuine potential.

As you become more comfortable with researching ideas and companies, ask yourself questions that can tell you whether further legwork is needed. These are some issues and questions to consider:

- Does the idea or trend you're researching seem to have long-term potential or is it more flash in the pan (like the mood ring or pet rock from the 1970s)?
- Is there a particular point of focus to the idea or does it offer potential in several different directions—and, if so, which of those directions appears most promising?
- Do you have personal experience with what you're researching? What about it do you find appealing or, by the same token, less than attractive?
- Is there an inherent flaw in the trend or development, such as price, availability, learning curve, or some other issue that may hinder its growth?
- Is the potential immediate or does it appear likely that development will be necessary over the course of a significant amount of time?
- How uniform is the coverage of the idea or development? Has it been universally praised or have others raised significant, telling misgivings?
- As to potential small-cap companies, are they bringing a genuinely new approach to an issue, product, or problem?
- How long has the company been around? Do they have sufficient history to show that they have achieved real progress?
- How much coverage has been given to a company? Has it been singled out by relatively few news sources or is it already a golden child of the media?
- What's the background of the company's officers? Have they had success in similar business ventures?

These are just a sampling of the questions you need to ask when performing initial research on small-cap companies. You are in the driver's seat; what you uncover and your interpretation of that information segue to the next logical step: building a systematic, comprehensive study of a small-cap stock itself. The focus of the following chapter begins this journey with an explanation of how to analyze the fundamentals.

The Bottom Line

- Picking winning small-cap stocks requires familiarity with what a company does, how its products are perceived, and an outlook for future growth prospects.
- What you buy, where you shop, and the products you use can be helpful in identifying potential small-cap stock investments.
- Significant economic, political, and social developments may signal new opportunities. China's hosting of the Olympics, the credit crunch, and the jump in oil prices are all examples of events that point to new investing opportunities.
- Use stock screening tools to pare down 7,000-plus companies into a manageable list of small-cap stocks with strong performance and attractive valuations.
- Check websites and publications to help your investigation of small-cap stocks with investment potential.
- When looking at small caps, ask the right questions to gauge their potential.
- Check whether the market as a whole has noticed what the company is doing, and raised the valuation as a result.

CHAPTER 4

Understanding and Evaluating Financial Statements

"The investor of today does not profit from yesterday's growth."
—Warren Buffett

"In the business world, the rearview mirror is always clearer than the windshield."
—Warren Buffett

"You don't make money by investing in a good company... You make money by investing in a company that is better than the market thinks."
—Robert Vishny, Institutional Investor

Financial statements are the scorecard of a public company. They provide investors with numbers and metrics that allow them to understand the top and bottom line performance of their investment. Through financial statements, you can compare the performance of your stocks with other companies and also look at quarter-over-quarter or year-over-year comparisons to determine whether the company is growing and improving, or facing challenges in its business.

Some public companies have aggressive managers and PR folk who like to paint a rosy picture of the future, discussing new initiatives, product launches, and partnerships. But ultimately, all of this good news should translate into revenues, earnings, and cash flow. The financial statements are meant to keep a company and its managers honest. For most public companies, financial reporting does just that—provides investors with a straightforward read on the company's financial performance every three months (the SEC requires most companies to file quarterly financial results within 35 days of the end of the quarter).

With small-cap stocks, it is often the story of the company and their prospects for the future that attract you to a potential investment. Earlier in this book, I explained how to identify industries or sectors poised for rapid growth, as well as ways to find strong small-cap stocks with a lot of promise. Now it is time to evaluate their financial performance by measuring financial results.

It is important to try to find small companies that are growing and appear on track for rapid expansion. But as an investor, you are buying more than a story; you are buying a company and becoming an owner of a small piece of a business. For this reason, understanding and evaluating the financial performance of every potential investment is absolutely required. And checking up on your portfolio of stocks every quarter is highly advisable if you want to maximize profits while minimizing risks.

Financial statements are often overlooked by individual investors because they are thought to be too complicated, too extensive, and sometimes intentionally or unintentionally misleading. They are lengthy and full of numbers, terms, and details that can be downright overwhelming and boring. But the fact is that there are only a few things you need to look at to understand the financial performance and identify red flags that could tip you off to financial misdeeds, manipulation, or outright fraud.

Looking at the most recent financial results, both annual and quarterly, is a good starting point. You begin by examining these results compared with those a year prior. The key thing to be looking for is improvements year-over-year. Revenues, earnings, and EPS should be growing, profit margins expanding, and cash increasing. It is also useful to look for longer-term trends to better understand the historical performance of a company and put the more recent results in context.

This chapter explains how financial statements are prepared and how you can evaluate them to make informed decisions. Positive signals in long-term trends include:

- Consistent growth of revenues.
- Equally consistent growth of net profits at a faster rate of growth than revenue growth, demonstrating the scalability of the business.
- Expanding profit margins.
- Footnotes that make sense and are not overly technical.
- Little or no difference between net earnings and *core* net earnings (core earnings is a concept developed by Standard & Poor's, reporting income from only the company's core activity and excluding non-core, non-repetitive items like capital gains, currency exchange profit or loss, accounting adjustments, and profit or loss resulting from acquisitions and mergers).

In this chapter, I explain:

- Generally Accepted Accounting Principles and the Basics of Accruals.
- Three components of a financial statement:
  - Balance sheet;
  - Income statement; and
  - Statement of cash flows.
- Ten key metrics you need to know.
- Earnings and variations on the different definitions involved.
- Cash flow and how it relates to earnings.
- Ten important accounting red flags that could signal a bad investment.

Generally Accepted Accounting Principles and the Basics of Accrual Accounting

There is no easy way to make accounting interesting. But this is the boring background information that explains the basis for accounting used by public companies.

Generally Accepted Accounting Principles (GAAP) consist of the common accounting guidelines and methods that companies are required to use when compiling their financial statements. But they're not just stipulated procedures; GAAP also represents the accepted way that firms report their financial condition. It's meant to be the way things are done.

GAAP is no singular auditing manual, but rather it is a series of opinions, rulings, and publications from several sources, led mostly by the American Institute of Certified Public Accountants (AICPA) and the Financial Accounting Standards Board (FASB).

On the surface, that makes perfect sense. GAAP provides consistency and objectivity between companies. If everyone plays by the same reporting rules, investors can accurately compare one company with another, certain that the guidelines ensure that they are judging one apple against another apple.

A benchmark of modern accounting practice is the accrual system. This system allows companies to book revenues and expenses by accrual, meaning transactions are recognized in the period in which they occur. This is different than cash accounting, which is often the way non-public small businesses track financials.

Accruals are used in four specific cases:

1. *Revenue has been earned but not yet received.* In this situation, which happens in most businesses, the journal entry sets up a current asset

under accounts receivable and offsets it with an increase to revenues. When the money is actually received, it is recorded as an increase to cash and a decrease to accounts receivable. This sets up earned income in the proper accounting period even though it has not yet been paid.

2. *Revenue has been received before it was earned.* In this situation, a customer prepays and the money is received. But because it is early, it is unearned income and has to be deferred to the future period. So the journal entry records it as an increase to cash and offsets that as a deferred credit, which shows up in the liability section of the balance sheet. Later, when the period arrives in which the income is supposed to be recorded, a journal entry eliminates the deferred credit and sets up the revenue.

3. *Accrued expenses or costs.* In this case, a company incurs an expense and owes money to a vendor in the current period, but it is not going to be paid until the next period. So a journal entry is set up to report current liabilities for each accrued expense situation, offset by a current-period expense or direct cost. In the following period when the bill is paid, it is recorded as a reduction to cash and also as an offsetting reduction to the current liability account.

4. *Prepaid expenses or costs.* When a company pays a bill early, it is not incurred until the following period. In this case, the initial payment is set up as an asset called prepaid expenses and offset as a reduction to cash. When the proper accounting period arrives, the reversing journal eliminates the prepaid asset and shows an increase in the expense account.

Accruals are essential to accurate reporting and recording of revenues, costs, and expenses. In certain situations, high levels of accruals translate to a misleading picture of the company's financial status. This can be particularly true with small-cap stocks, those fast-growing companies prone to volatile earnings. No matter how well-managed, companies will have periods when growth slows, often considerably. And that is tempting to management trying to attract institutional as well as individual investors. Knowing that everyone likes predictability, a volatile report can scare away investors, so the temptation to manipulate outcomes is certainly there. This demonstrates why it is so important for you to focus on long-term earnings trends rather than one or two quarters in isolation when evaluating a small-cap stock.

The vast majority of financial managers approach the challenge of accrual accounting with skill and integrity. They are very good at accurately reporting transactions and trying to keep incurred and earned transactions in their proper time slot. They make no attempt to glaze over or shield results.

That sort of integrity is found in the majority of accountants who, as a rule, certainly do not want to go to jail on fraud charges. But high standards are not universal. Given the leeway in GAAP and the opportunity to misuse the accrual system, managers bent on chicanery can easily set up deceptive earnings outcomes rather than striving for a completely accurate reporting system. Although manipulation eventually catches up with a company, the deception can be continued for many years, even with the complicity of outside auditors.

Keep in mind, GAAP is a set of *guidelines*, and some companies and auditing firms simply do not adhere to them consistently or interpret these guidelines differently. Making matters even more difficult, auditors in supposedly independent firms do not always find these inconsistencies or when they do, they negotiate with management.

GAAP allows for a great deal of leeway in how financial data are compiled and presented, and this lets company financial officers argue their case with their auditors. There is a lot of flexibility in the rules, and as long as a company can find an opinion, interpretation, or justification for their position, the auditor will often just go along with it.

Financial Statements Made Simple

Every quarter, publicly traded companies file their financial reports with the SEC and release their performance to the public. These statements include the balance sheet, income statement, and cash flow statement. Each of these components of the financial statement is interconnected, with the numbers in one component affecting the others. Let's briefly examine these components of a financial statement, and discuss the importance of each.

Balance Sheet: The balance sheet is a summary of the ending balances of assets and liabilities at the close of the period. This is what is meant by the *balance* part of the balance sheet. The balance sheet shows investors the value of the hard assets of a company—office space, equipment, supplies, and inventory. It also shows assets, such as cash, and liabilities that include short-term debt, long-term debt, and accounts payable.

Information on this statement is used to measure the actual cash the business has on hand and determine if it has enough cash to continue to sustain operations, in the event the company loses money from operations. Even profitable businesses can burn through cash. Cash is considered the lifeblood of a company—required to fund operations and growth initiatives. If a company doesn't have enough cash on hand

and business conditions change, things can turn south quickly. Simply put, cash is king.

Important distinctions on the balance sheet are between current and long-term categories of accounts. Current assets are those assets in the form of cash or that are convertible to cash within 12 months (cash, accounts, and notes receivable net of reserves for bad debts), as well as the cost of inventory. Long-term assets include capital assets like buildings, vehicles, machinery, and equipment, and net of accumulated depreciation (the value of depreciation written off as expenses each year).

Current liabilities are all debts owed within 12 months, including accounts and taxes payable and the payments due on long-term debts over the next 12 months. Long-term liabilities include all debts payable beyond the next 12 months.

Measuring the company's working capital is essential. A popular balance sheet ratio is called the current ratio: the sum of current assets divided by the sum of current liabilities. As a general standard, the resulting ratio should be two or better. This often demonstrates that there is enough cash on hand to pay current bills, as well as accounts convertible to cash within a year to pay for upcoming obligations.

For companies with large inventories, the quick assets ratio is used instead of the current ratio. This is calculated in the same manner, but excludes the asset value of inventory. The standard for the quick assets ratio is one or higher. This is appropriate to avoid distortion from the current ratio because the company has a large investment in its inventory. By ignoring inventory and focusing on cash, the quick assets ratio presents a better measure of true working capital for companies whose inventory levels are kept high from necessity throughout the year.

An equally important balance sheet ratio used to judge cash flow is called the debt ratio, a comparison between long-term debt and total capitalization. (The definition of "total" capitalization is the sum of long-term debts and shareholders' equity.) To calculate, divide the long-term debt balance by the total capitalization. If you see the percentage of debt growing over time, this is a red flag. The more long-term debt a company is carrying, the more future earnings have to go toward repayment of the debt plus interest, and the less is left over to fund growth or pay dividends.

Income Statement: The income statement shows sales, costs associated with the products or services, overhead, and the bottom line—what is left over after all expenses. This is the most important component of the financial statement. The sales of a company, also known as the revenues, measure the ability of the organization to sell products or services. Revenues are the first line item on the income statement, and this is the first place to look for growth. Buying companies that are presales is a sucker's game—even venture capitalists try to stay away from most of these opportunities. They are just too unproven and difficult to evaluate.

Other key things to look at on the income statement are gross profit, net profit, and earnings per share. Gross income shows the net difference between revenues and cost of goods sold, or profit before deducting operating expenses. The general expenses are deducted next, resulting in net operating profit or loss. This is further adjusted for non-operating income and expenses and tax liabilities, and the bottom line is the net earnings and earnings per share. Also shown on the income statement is the number of shares of stock issued and outstanding, which can be used to calculate the market capitalization and earnings per share.

It is important to review these numbers in comparison to one another, by examining margins and growth rates. Gross profit is expressed as a percentage of revenues, as is the net profit. The dollar amount of each section of the statement should be in line with growth trends. The ideal situation involves steadily growing revenues, a consistent percentage of gross profit, and very little change in the dollar amount of expenses. Net profit should be consistent or growing gradually. One of the most common errors to watch out for occurs when a company begins growing in terms of revenue, but does not control expenses. So the expenses outpace revenue growth, reducing profit margins. Be especially wary when expenses grow because management is increasing their compensation, meaning earnings get eroded even with revenue growth; this is one the biggest red flags on the income statement that can indicate mismanagement.

All analysis of the income statement should be compared with the previous comparable time period (year or quarter) in order to have context, and a multi-year review of the income statement trends is a smart idea. I like to see revenues growing, gross profits remaining stable or gradually improving over time, expenses decreasing as a percentage of sales, net income growing, and profit margins expanding.

Cash Flow Statement: The statement of cash flows tracks the movement of cash in and out of the business through operations, financings, and other purchases or sales of assets. Cash flows simply measure the ability of a company to generate cash through various activities. Since we know cash is the lifeblood of a company, it is important to examine how a company converts revenues into cash and then reinvests that cash to grow the business and generate a return for shareholders.

The income statement ties in to the statement of cash flows, and is the first line item. It is then adjusted for non-cash income and expenses (accruals and depreciation, for example), resulting in a sub-total for cash-basis income from operations. This is increased by additional sources of cash (such as loan proceeds, investment profits, financing activities, and money from the sale of capital assets).

Once the total sources of funds are identified, the next section shows the reductions (applications) of funds. These include the purchase of capital assets, repayments of long-term loans, payment of dividends to stockholders, funds paid to a pension or profit-sharing plan, or payments for acquisitions of other companies.

The bottom line of the statement is the net increase or decrease in cash. The net change in cash defines the effectiveness of management's ability to generate cash to fund the business. I like to invest in companies that are growing their cash through profitable operations, and not raising funds through increasing debt or issuing new stock. Most small-cap companies fund their growth through the issuance of equity, while some will use a line of credit for short-term cash needs or borrow money from a bank for longer-term debt. Very few small caps issue bonds in the form of long-term debt. However, if a company is increasing long-term financing, that alone isn't a bad thing; it simply means higher future debt service and interest expense. By the same argument, issuing new shares of stock dilutes existing shareholders, so that current shareholder value is eroded. If total cash is decreasing, this can mean that the company will be in trouble down the road if they aren't able to improve profits and curb money-losing operations. Healthy companies are self-sustaining and do not depend on raising more money through debt or equity to fund operations.

Investors in small caps are buying the future earnings of a company. If those earnings don't exist or are not turning into cash, than you need to question the value of the proposed investment.

Many investors don't appreciate the connection between the three statements, and they focus exclusively on the income statement. While the income statement is one important component, it is not everything. The balance sheet and statement of cash flows are important checks on the financial health of a business, beyond the review of revenues, expenses, and income. The workings of these statements and their results are derived from accrual accounting.

Ten Key Metrics to Review in Every Financial Statement

The trend is your friend, as the old Wall Street adage tells us. And this is certainly true. I would prefer to review ten years of solid financial growth versus 12 months. However, when it comes to buying small caps poised for significant growth, we want to find unknown stocks. Companies with a two-year, five-year, or especially 10-year history of consistent financial growth have either grown beyond the definition of small cap, have become widely known and already had their share price rise accordingly, or have a serious underlying problem that is the reason they remain out of favor.

Successful small-cap investors must often focus on those companies with a limited track record of success. The company whose success is widely known and have consistently put up impressive numbers year in and year out have share prices and valuations that reflect this consistent outperformance. It is the small caps that have just begun turning a profit, achieved an unexpected turnaround, or launched an innovative product that will put some serious growth into the business that we as investors seek out; it is these companies on the verge of greatness that deserve our valuable investments, and will reward us should our thesis be proven correct.

Knowing that more often than not we as small-cap investors are working with a limited history of relevant financial performance, here are 10 critical metrics to review:

1. *Revenues.* Reported revenues are the heart of every business. If the company can't sell products or services, there isn't really much more you need to look at. Look for companies with regularly increasing revenues and a steady or increasing rate of growth. Stagnant revenues mean the company isn't innovative, gaining market share, or growing; declines in revenue mean the business is doomed and others are taking market share. Seek out not only companies that are growing sales, but also those whose sales growth outpaces competitors within the industry. The best are those whose rate of growth is increasing as the company becomes larger.

2. *Net income.* Net income, or profits, is what is left over after all of the bills are paid. Just like revenue, you want to see growth in net income and, if possible, increases in the rate of growth. Unprofitable companies are a big risk. If you can't make money, you shouldn't be in business, and definitely shouldn't be public (there are of course exceptions to this rule, such as biotech companies that require significant capital investment in the early years to invest in R&D). A growing company can realistically create greater rates of return every year, but at the point where maximum effectiveness in the market has been reached, the percentage of net profit should level out while the dollar amount of revenues and profits should continue to grow. For example, one of the greatest stories in American stocks has been Wal-Mart, which started as a small personal store and grew to the largest retail company in the world. Wal-Mart reports an amazingly consistent growth in revenues every year, as well as a surprisingly consistent net profit, usually

between 3.1 percent and 3.3 percent every year on revenues in the tens of billions, which is a sign of incredibly effective internal control.

3. *Growth: revenue and net income.* As important as revenues and profits are individually, a third crucial trend is the combined tracking of revenue and profit growth over several quarters and years. You want to see growing revenue dollar volume with consistent or growing net earnings. You need both. This is why the most important income statement test involves two forms of analysis regarding these two line items. First, you need to see ever-higher revenues with steady rates of return in earnings. Second, you also want to track the rate of growth from one year to the next in both revenues and earnings. These are supposed to move along a similar scale. So, for example, if the company you are studying has been reporting 25 percent per year increase in revenues over the previous year, you should see a similar 20 percent increase in net income.

4. *Gross margin.* A company's gross margin is the amount left over when you subtract the cost of goods sold from revenues. The proper standard for an "acceptable" gross margin depends on the industry and the kind of product it produces. For example, a hardware manufacturer will have a much lower gross margin than a software developer. (For big-company examples, compare IBM and Microsoft.) You should look for very consistent gross margins every year. The direct costs (materials purchased for manufacture or sale, direct labor, freight, and other direct costs) should not change between years unless the company undergoes some major restructuring changes. So if you do see a change, especially a decline in gross margin, it deserves examination and explaination.

5. *Current ratio.* Working capital is the lifeblood of every organization. So the current ratio (current assets divided by current liabilities) should be reported at very consistent levels every quarter (or, if a cyclical company, every year). The usual standard is for a current ratio of two or better, but many very strong industries report current ratio between one and two. For those companies with a lot invested in inventory—and notably, reporting big changes in inventory levels depending on the season—the quick assets ratio may be more reliable. This is the same as the current ratio, excluding inventory balances.

6. *Debt ratio.* The current ratio and quick assets ratio are only part of the working capital picture. The debt ratio tells you how much of the company's capitalization is made up of debt (long-term loans and bonds). It is computed by dividing the balance of long-term debt by total capitalization (long-term debt and shareholders' equity). As with most ratios, an acceptable percentage of long-term debt relies on the industry and the company's history. The most important aspect of the debt ratio is the trend. You want to see a very steady or falling debt ratio over many years. To see an example of a debt ratio out of control,

check General Motors and its 10-year history. The problems GM found itself in by 2008 were easily predicted many years before. By 2008, its debt ratio was above 100 percent, meaning there was a negative value to the company's book value or no real equity. This occurred because GM was losing money, increasing borrowings, and failing to fix its ever-growing problems. If you find the same trend in small caps, a large and growing debt load, you can anticipate big problems down the road.

7. *Combined current ratio and debt ratio.* The most important working capital test combines a study of current ratio and debt ratio. If you see a consistent current ratio in periods when the company is reporting net losses, you should be puzzled. It simply doesn't make sense. But at the same time, if the debt ratio is increasing and current assets are tracking even higher debt, it points out a serious red flag. The current ratio is meaningless by itself if the company is increasing its cash balances, accounts receivable, or inventory to maintain a good current ratio.

8. *Executive compensation.* It's an old story: A small company starts to succeed, revenues grow by leaps and bounds, and net earnings are spectacular. The stock price starts rising as well. And then, you notice, earnings begin leveling out, perhaps even falling. With growth in revenues, why are profits falling? Your answer, you might discover, is that the top executives are giving themselves big raises, valuable stock options, and bonuses. Look at the General and Administrative line item in the income statement, as this is where these expenses are included. What does this mean? As an investor, it means that management is taking your profits and benefiting from your market risk to reward themselves. It does not just happen at Enron or WorldCom, but among companies of all sizes. Keep an eye on executive compensation, and if you see earnings being converted to big paychecks for a few fat cats, get out before it's too late. Increased compensation and incentives such as stock options is appropriate for executives so long as it is justified by strong financial performance of the company.

9. *Dividend history.* Companies that are able to pay dividends consistently tend to be well-managed and effective in returning capital to shareholders. You have to have cash on hand to pay dividends. Those companies that have been able to increase dividends every year are the exceptions. One market analysis service (www.mergent.com) tracks what it calls *dividend achievers*, those companies whose dividend rate has increased every year for at least 10 years. A study of those companies reveals an interesting phenomenon. Virtually all of the companies have reported higher stock prices over the 10-plus-year period. Their revenue growth is consistent. And they are often either leaders in their industry sector or very competitive with other strongly managed companies. Dividends tend to be very unusual for small-cap stocks, as these companies

typically are more growth-oriented and executives prefer to reinvest earnings in projects that will contribute to future financial growth.

10. *Core earnings versus net income.* The S&P distinction of core earnings (earnings only from core activities) versus total earnings is an important one. You will notice that the less volatile, steadily growing companies also tend to have little or no core earnings adjustments. Companies with more inconsistent and erratic revenue and earnings histories tend to have much higher core earnings adjustments. The unreliability of earnings trends defines low quality of earnings.

What Exactly Are Earnings?

High-quality earnings are essential. The quality of a small-cap company's earnings means more than just the integrity of the numbers. First and foremost, earnings quality reflects on the company as a whole, including skillful management, competitive stance, and excellence of product and service. A company that adopts a conservative financial reporting policy is likely to carry over that attitude to every aspect of its operations. Can you genuinely make the same assumption about another company that is not above playing with its numbers to make things appear better than reality?

The integrity of earnings also carries over to your role as a prospective investor. Although there are some elements about a business that are more faith-based than empirical, earnings reports should not be one of them. If earnings are high quality, you have a much firmer foundation of knowledge about that company's current status as well as its prospects. On top of that, you can avoid companies whose exaggerated earnings eventually come back down to earth—and they always do—and, with them, the value of the company's stock.

Companies that are well-managed and solid don't have to manipulate numbers to make conditions seem better than they actually are. Even so, the pressure to meet estimates is always present, and you should always perform a deeper level of analysis when a firm "just meets" or "just beats" analyst estimates. Companies that are struggling may feel that they have no other choice. Taking a reverse perspective, conservative accounting practices—and the high-quality earnings that emanate from those practices—also put the company in a better position for the reporting of future earnings and growth in future stock prices. Not only are low-quality earnings unjustifiable, but companies that report them are taking potential future earnings out of play when they inflate today's results. And high-quality earnings are not merely more conservative; earnings in the future will also be accurate because all levels of revenues, and expenses are reported fairly and consistently. Conservative accounting cements a reliable trend and reporting pattern.

Earnings are the net profits from operations. There are three sub-totaled line items on an income statement that you should look at:

The first is "net income from operations" or "operating net income." This is the calculated profits including all revenues, minus direct costs and expenses related specifically to the core business. It is supposed to exclude nonrecurring or noncore sources of income, but history has demonstrated that some companies use a loose interpretation.

The second is "net pre-tax income," which adds other income and subtracts other expenses from operating income, but it does not include the liability for income taxes. Typically, these adjustments include interest income and expense, currency exchange profit or loss, capital gains and losses, payments or receipts in settled or finalized lawsuits, and other non-recurring, non-core transactions.

The third takes the net pre-tax income and deducts the liability for federal income taxes (state and local taxes are already deducted in the expense section of the report). This can be a big number. As of 2009, corporations can be required to pay up to 38 percent of their net income in federal taxes.

An exceptionally conservative version of earnings would exclude non-core earnings completely. This is a worthwhile variation when presented in a side-by-side comparison with the more traditional form of earnings. It would show wide disparity when non-core earnings remained in earnings, or when management changes accounting assumptions that distort reported profits. You can spot trends over many years, but core income-based earnings alongside the traditional calculation is even more revealing. This calculation, sometimes called *ongoing earnings*, isolates core earnings in an attempt to purify the long-term trend of core activity; this recognizes that nonrecurring and noncore forms of profit and loss distort financial statements and bring down quality of earnings to the most unreliable level.

Another variation is called *pro forma earnings*. The term pro forma refers to estimates of future activity; so just as the price-to-earnings (P/E) ratio may be described as "forward P/E" (based on estimates of earnings in the coming year), earnings may be prepared on a similar pro forma (estimated) basis. Using estimates for financial ratios is always a troubling idea. Just as you may have heard that a verbal contract isn't worth the paper it's written on, the same is true of financial estimates. They aren't worth any more than the subjective opinion of the person developing the forecast.

Another variation of pro forma earnings adjusts the reported earnings to exclude some expenses. For example, if a company sells off a big segment of its operations, and that segment had lost money throughout the year, an argument can be made for excluding its net losses. The loss distorts earnings and, because the company no longer owns that segment, the rationale for using pro forma and leaving out the loss can be made. It more accurately reflects earnings trends going forward. Even though this is acceptable if used sparingly, any adjustments to the actual numbers can be troubling, because they are easily misused, distorting earnings and ruining the quality of earnings as a result.

A more obscure variety is called *headline earnings*, which is defined as the current estimated earnings based on a press release, rumor, or news story, good or bad. For example, a drug company may announce that it is anticipating FDA approval for a new drug that is estimated to double its profits. If true, the headline earnings is accurate, but if the approval does not happen, then the headline is just that, a headline. Another example was seen in 2008 for Apple Computer when Steve Jobs, losing weight at an alarming level, was rumored to be dying; it was then announced he had a vitamin deficiency and was doing well, yet not long after that he took an extended leave of absence. The headlines in this case took Apple shares up and down even more than the volatile bear market, pointing out the company's vulnerability to the fortunes of one person, but also creating a lot of headline earnings changes.

The *cash earnings* are calculated by dividing earnings before interest, taxes, depreciation, and amortization (EBITDA) by diluted shares outstanding. EBITDA is often a preferred way to calculate earnings for a company, because it excludes many non-core business calculations (interest, taxes, depreciation, and amortization). By excluding these items, EBITDA is designed to give a true picture of the cash flow being generated by a company. By isolating cash or core income, you get a purer version of income for evaluation. The trend in cash earnings can often be more revealing and provide a better version of quality of earnings than the more complex, polluted traditional variation.

Ultimately, the test of quality is going to be defined as the sustainability of earnings. How capably is the company going to be able to create a positive revenue and earnings trend and continue that trend into the future? This question has to be qualified. It is realistic to expect a company to continue a high quality of earnings when it maintains the same percentage of net earnings every year even while the dollar amounts rise. It is less realistic to expect the percentage to continue to increase every year indefinitely. Given the inescapable levels of cost of goods sold and expenses, there is always a reasonable limit to the net yield. For most investors, it is glowing enough when management can report consistent net return while revenues rise each and every year.

The Quality Gap in GAAP: High- versus Low-Quality Earnings

None of the analysis of financial statements is simple. In fact, the best you can hope for is a consistent and honest attempt to accurately report transactions. That sounds easy, but it is not. Accounting is complicated and involves a lot of interpretation, and this is where mischief can easily rise to the surface. And the GAAP rules leave a wide margin for interpretation of virtually any and all of the numbers.

One broad example of this is found in the disparity between high-quality earnings and low-quality earnings. High-quality earnings are the product of conservative accounting practices that provide a clear and reliable picture of the company's financial status. You spot high-quality earnings in several ways:

- The trend in earnings is growing consistently over many years.
- Earnings track growth in revenues consistently, without questionable increases in earnings that exceed the rate of revenue growth.
- A company with high-quality earnings tends to move up on the competitive ladder within a sector, indicating that those earnings are accompanied by a strong core business.
- The dollar level of earnings increases each year, and the net return (percentage of net to revenues) remains consistent or grows over time.

Low-quality earnings are just the opposite—earnings that have been buffed up through liberal accounting procedures that, in turn, do not portray the company in a fully accurate light. Some symptoms include:

- High volatility, with earnings increasing and decreasing each year.
- Unexplained variation in the net return over time.
- Big core earnings adjustments to reported net earnings.
- Disparity between reported earnings and P/E when the number of outstanding shares has not changed (indicating the possibility of manipulation in reported outcome to affect the stock price artificially).
- Significant one-time expenses that regularly distort the performance of the business.

For example, if a company reports ever-growing revenues over a decade, with a corresponding growth in net earnings, it makes a strong case that the quality of those earnings is high. In comparison, a company whose revenue history is erratic and whose yearly earnings are offset with periods of large losses cannot make as strong a case. It is impossible to decide whether the company's coming years are going to show growth or profit, and so their quality of earnings is quite low. Remember, investors like certainty, and one attribute of low quality earnings is the inability to rely on a trend continuing into the future.

How do earnings fit into the larger picture? A reliable way to critique a company and its financial results is by comparing it to other companies in the same sector, studying trends over many years when data are available, and analyzing outcomes in all kinds of markets. This approach gives you actionable intelligence because it demonstrates how quality earnings act within the larger market. Some generalizations worth remembering:

- Companies run with integrity report better numbers over time.
- Companies employing conservative accounting decisions reflect reliable and consistent trends in the fundamentals.
- Strong quality of earnings often translates to growing strength within a sector, meaning small-cap companies with quality earnings tend to grow faster than the average.

Of course, because these are generalizations, they do not apply in each and every case. Every investor operates from some variation of a model expected to produce reliable results. The model may limit the sectors studied, capitalization size preferences, focus on attributes of management, or actual financial trends. One of the most reliable business models is incorporation of quality of earnings within three important aspects: reliable and honest reporting, conservative accounting policies, and exceptional performance relative to the sector at large.

There is a significant difference between low-quality earnings and fraudulent earnings. Low-quality earnings may be nothing more than the result of poor management, aggressive accounting, or even rapid expansion. Fraud is more extreme, usually the result of outright and intentional falsification of the results. The numbers are consciously altered to obscure the true financial status of a company—criminal activity, pure and simple.

For example, depreciation is a non-cash expense set up to estimate a recovery period for a capital asset. The IRS publishes a recommended depreciation method for each class of asset, but that is not always the most conservative or accurate way to actually calculate depreciation. Under IRS rules, some asset classes can be depreciated using accelerated methods, meaning that more deductions are allowed in the earlier years of a recovery period, and less later on. But companies can also elect to use a more conservative straight-line method, in which the same amount is deducted every year, and in some cases, the recovery period can even be extended.

Remembering that the law allows the use of accelerated depreciation, is it always the best method to use? Some assets within a single class might realistically decline in value rapidly in their early life. For example, computers tend to become obsolete quickly and may be appropriately depreciated as quickly as possible. But office furniture is more likely to last many years more, and it could be accurate and conservative to use the straight-line method. Frustrating management's attempts at applying depreciation rules fairly, the elections allowed require that the decision be applied to *all* assets in each recovery period for the specific year those assets are placed into service. So if management invests in two different kinds of capital assets in the same year, a judgment call requires a decision that has to be applied to all of those investments.

The depreciation example is a fairly straightforward one. It is not easy to decide which alternative is more accurate or more reflective of the truth. Accounting decisions like this and, on a more complex level, make financial statements the result of many difficult judgment calls. For example, setting the value of currency exchange profits or losses, valuation of marketable securities, picking the level of a bad debt reserve, methods for valuing inventory, placing book value on unexercised stock options, estimating the book value of pension assets, and many similar decisions all may affect the reported earnings for every company. What you need to look for in a small cap is management that truly does struggle with the question of how to make accurate interpretations. Avoid companies that explain their decisions with obscure language and are unwilling or unable to tell you what those decisions mean, and that seem to always make decisions that favor their earnings in a positive manner (even when that means being inconsistent from one year to the next).

Evaluating the quality of earnings is elusive simply because all of those accounting decisions affect earnings directly, and many affect it significantly. So management has an array of temptations to deal with, and some managers give in to these temptations. The rewards of quality earnings are great, and include attracting institutional investors to buy the stock, bonuses and additional compensation for executives, and ultimately a higher share price. You could also define *quality of earnings* by describing quality of management as people who strive to provide accurate and consistent reports.

Different variations of earnings can make the reported outcome different than what you expect, and this naturally leads to the possibility of manipulation. So quality of earnings requires consistency in how important outcomes like earnings are calculated.

The basic formula is well-known, but just as quality of earnings refers to the integrity of the numbers, quality of earnings refers to consistency of calculations. If variations are used, those should be disclosed, but unfortunately, they are not always laid out for all to see. Financial reporters, analysts working for a firm underwriting a new issue, or paid analysts can easily adjust earnings to make an outcome look better than it is. In the small-cap world, where growth is exponential and rapid in many cases, even minor adjustments can mislead you, whether intentional or not.

Under GAAP, the calculation of earnings may be legal but inaccurate. So GAAP earnings may include estimates or accounting outcomes that meet statutory requirements but not tax requirements. Thus, the statutory and tax basis of reported income are quite different, and of course so is earnings. This disparity arises because earnings is often reported on the market quite soon after a quarter or fiscal year has ended, but this may be many months before an audit is completed, meaning that audit-adjusted earnings might be vastly different than earnings highlighted in the news stories. By the time this is adjusted, it is a distant accounting adjustment and footnote to the more recent report. The problem is even more glaring for quarterly financial statements. These are not subject to the very detailed annual audit of a publicly-listed company, so management has great leeway in estimating the quarterly results.

Investment Research: Can It Be Trusted?

Many individual investors depend on investment research to help them with their personal investment decisions. The investment research business has been through lots of changes in recent years, and the collapse of Wall Street in 2008 and 2009 will lead to more evolution of this industry that many investors depend upon.

One simple fact that any investor would be foolish to discount is that investment research invariably costs money. To provide research, firms need to generate revenues to cover those research costs. This reality makes earnings calculations even more complicated. How a firm generates revenues to cover research costs could provide a window into the credibility of their analysts' ratings. Today, there are four basic business models of investment research, each with its own unique way of creating pitfalls for investors.

Trading Revenue-Based Model: The trading revenue-based model is employed by brokerage houses and relies on commissions generated on trades to support research. Revenues being derived from trading commissions can create problems in and of themselves. One obvious problem is that little effort is dedicated to covering firms with smaller market capitalization with thinly traded shares, simply because there's little to be made in the way of trading commissions. This explains why a firm such as Microsoft has 30 analysts covering it this year and some of the firms you'll see me cover through SmallCapInvestor.com have none. Another problem built into this model is that frequently changing ratings on stocks in the form of upgrades and downgrades can increase trading volume and thereby increase revenues.

Investment Banking Model: The investment banking model is one in which firms provide research coverage on companies with whom they have investment banking relationships (or those with whom they wish to establish such relationships). In the late 1990s, there were numerous independent, boutique investment banks whose analysts covered a wide range of companies. Some of these boutiques focused on emerging small caps and technology stocks, and could support robust research departments. But with

IPOs falling out of favor, and consolidation within the industry in the last decade, many of these boutique firms have disappeared, and with them their research coverage of some of the smaller publicly-traded companies. Investment banking relationships can prove to be very lucrative and may mean the analyst's firm is underwriting the sale of equity or debt now or sometime in the future. In this and most any case, client companies would obviously prefer favorable research reports. Additionally, positive reports go a long way to attracting new investment banking clients. Clearly, one can see how conflicts of interest can arise with this model, which was the de-facto standard in the late 1990's pre-Sarbanes Oxley.

Paid Research: Paid research is a newer model and one in which a public company pays a research firm for coverage. More and more small-cap companies are employing this method to increase their exposure and spur investment. With this model, it's rather easy for one to imagine that a company wouldn't want to pay for an unfavorable rating, and thus the concern is that by paying for research coverage, companies are buying favorable ratings. Many small-cap stocks that wish to have analyst coverage but are unable to attract investment bank analysts to cover their stock will resort instead to the paid research alternative.

Subscription Research and Investment Newsletters: Subscription research or investment newsletters are a type of research whereby the individual investors pays a subscription fee for a firm's research service or investment advisory. The advantage for the individual investor is that there is often greater transparency between the firm providing the research and the investment being evaluated. The downside is that the investor pays the fee for the research. However, in a world where money is on the line, the accurate evaluation of investments is most important. Of the four models, the subscription model inherently creates the most impartial environment. Newsletters including my SmallCapInvestor.com PRO service depend upon subscribers to support the research of small-cap stocks and investment opportunities.

A Quality Test: Cash Flow Instead of Earnings

An obscure but valuable test you can perform yourself is a variation of the earnings per share (EPS) trend. Calculate operating cash flow per share instead of reported earnings per share. This is advantageous for several reasons. First, management cannot tinker with cash; it either is in the bank or it is not, and paid or still owed.

"Operating cash flow" means the cash generated from the operations of the company, defined as revenue minus all expenses. It is often calculated at EBITDA. Divide that dollar value by the number of outstanding shares to find CPS (cash-flow per share). If this outcome is higher than EPS, it can be interpreted to mean that quality of earnings is positive. Why? Because the company has managed to generate more cash than its reported profit.

A sensible way to apply CPS to analyze quality of earnings is to track it along with EPS as part of a comprehensive analysis of the balance sheet and income statement. So you would remove any noncore, nonrecurring items and also adjust for increases in long-term liabilities. Only by doing these adjustments can you rely on the CPS outcome and use it as a confirming indicator next to earnings for long-term quality of earnings.

The Enron Saga

If you need a good example of how financial statements can be manipulated, I only need to give you one word: Enron. Although Enron was not a small-cap stock when its troubles came to light, the problems disclosed are instructive and can serve as an objective lesson on why you need to be careful when relying on financial statements.

In hindsight, the name is synonymous with a vast array of unsavory doings. Once esteemed as a big player in the big business of energy, Enron was a disaster, and its management fooled many people. Those deceived include the Dow Jones Company, which added Enron to its prestigious Dow Jones Utility Average (and then quickly removed it once the real problems were disclosed). Enron, indeed, turned out to be a house of cards. Thousands of jobs lost, and billions of market capitalization evaporated in a short period of time, wiping out the investment accounts of employees and investors. Reputations, careers, and lives were devastated.

What started as a legitimate energy pipeline company that turned out big profits for years, Enron altered its numbers to continue reporting ever-greater profits and stock price, reporting inflated and non-existent profits through intentional and illegal accounting tricks. The greed of management drove a series of bad decisions to report growth where there simply was none. Remember, investors love growth. Wall Street analysts and investors want to see consistent improvements in the key financial metrics, including revenues, net income, EPS, gross margins, and cash flow.

And, boiling it down to its essence, the debacle that was Enron largely focused on bookkeeping—or, more accurately, bookkeeping whose sole reason for existence was to hide the financial iceberg that Enron was doomed to strike. Making matters worse, Enron's auditing firm of Arthur Andersen, once hailed as beyond reproach, was charged with conspiring to help Enron hide the truth, a fact that led to the dissolution of the entire auditing company.

Here are the details, in a nutshell: Enron created offshore entities, units used primarily to avoid taxes and to hide operating losses. They also provided the company's principals and managers with full anonymity that would shield the massive losses. As with many lies, small ones spawned larger ones, which then made it necessary to cover up more. The idea was to make Enron look more profitable than it actually was; moreover, the scheme created a maelstrom in which corporate officers went deeper and deeper into deception every quarter to foster the illusion of billions in profits while the company was bleeding losses.

For a while, it worked. Enron's stock soared. Company executives leveraged the inflated price to cash in their stock options and sell the stock, making them millions in gains that were used to buy multimillion dollar homes in Houston's nicest neighborhoods as well as vacation homes around the country. This all occurred because Enron executives were lured by incentive compensation. Their annual bonuses and options were all tied to profits and stock price levels, so they had a direct financial incentive to lie.

Yet another problem was the involvement of ambitious partners in Arthur Andersen's Houston offices. Originally, the firm was known for its ethical standards (founder Andersen himself was once fired by a client for refusing to cook the books; that company went out of business soon after, but this set the tone for Andersen as the *most ethical* of the public auditing firms). However, in more recent times, management changed the rules and instituted a requirement that all auditing partners had to bring in two dollars of non-audit revenue for every dollar earned from audits. This made it increasingly difficult for auditors to blow the whistle and, in the case of Enron, put the partner right in bed with the false statements prepared by Enron.

Some revisionists have tried to portray the Enron story as an unfortunate series of poor decisions. The ugly truth was, while Enron insiders knew all too well that the company was teetering on financial collapse, the company's investors were kept completely in the dark.

We all know too well how that little tableau played out. But, within the devastation that Enron wrought, there's a vital lesson for everyone, including small-cap investors. For all the importance that we place on the numbers and reports companies are required to provide, there are many ways to make all that data appear far rosier than it is, and many of those ways are all too easily manipulated.

Ten Accounting Red Flags

You do not have to get an advanced accounting degree to master some
of the basics of financial analysis. It is very productive to (1) know how
manipulation takes place, (2) identify the trends showing that something
manipulative is going on, and (3) understand the questions to ask.

Ten important red flags to watch out for:

1. *Unusual accounts receivables growth.* If accounts receivables are growing at a faster pace than the company's sales, this can indicate that the
   company is making bad sales to companies unable or unwilling to pay,
   which could result in bad debt down the road. It may also indicate
   that the company is booking revenues before the proper time, one of
   the most common practices within the universe of manipulation. Future
   sales are simply recognized early, inflating earnings. The tell-tale sign,
   of course, is accounts receivable growth in excess of reported revenue
   levels. Studying the dollar amounts is not adequate to spot this. Instead,
   compare the rate of growth in year-to-year revenues and receivables.
2. *Unusual deferrals on the balance sheet.* If you spot an item under the
   assets section called "prepaid assets" or "deferred assets," take a closer
   look. This could be a sign that the company has created artificial revenues with a simple journal entry: crediting revenues and setting up a
   prepaid or deferred asset. An explanation could justify this, but it has
   to make sense. For example, an entry could be justified with this explanation: "Setting up revenues under contract with a major customer
   as earned in the current year but scheduled to be paid over a five-year
   period per contract." As long as this explanation can be documented,
   it should be accepted. However, to represent earned income in the
   current year, there must be a delivery of the goods or services in the
   current year. Also look for more dubious explanations, remembering
   that if it doesn't make sense, it is probably not for real. For example,
   "Setting up deferral in anticipation of current-period earnings not yet
   booked and long-term in nature, pending completion of international
   provision agreement with subsidiaries and with major customers." What
   does this mean? The company has made no effort to prove that these
   revenues are for real, so they probably are not. Booking current year
   revenues for long-term deferral occurs, but it is unusual.
3. *Falsifying actual revenue earned.* The previous kinds of revenue reporting are often based on actual revenue to be earned in the future.
   It manipulates the facts by showing the revenue before it is actually
   earned. However, another kind of manipulation involves simply making up revenue and reporting it. For example, a company may receive
   loan proceeds and, instead of reporting these proceeds as a liability,
   set it up as cash revenue. A similar problem arises when a company

sells investments and instead of reporting net investment income, the full value of the sale is reported as current income. For example, in 1989, Cineplex Odeon reported revenue from selling off a production company. This transformed what would have been a $14.5 million loss for the year into a $48 million reported net income. Treating the sale as revenue was deceptive because it was actually a nonrecurring capital gain. The reported sale distorted the true picture and violated the accounting standards for this kind of transaction.

4. *Capitalizing current year expenses.* Another favorite way to manipulate earnings is by capitalizing some current year expenses. This sets up a prepaid or deferred asset instead of reporting the expense itself, boosting current year earnings. The idea is to write off these prepaid expenses over several years, but once a company starts artificially increasing net earnings, it tends to only get worse over time. It is not normal to set up expenses and amortize them over many years; some exceptions include payment of a three-year insurance premium and amortizing it over the following 36 months, and similar, easily explained cases. But when the prepaid amount is quite high and remains unexplained or explained poorly, it could be a form of manipulation.

5. *Sugar bowling.* This is the practice of deferring some revenue until future years. When a company has an unusually successful year, it may sugar bowl some of those earnings to offset lower results in the future. This is also called "cookie jar" accounting, and as cute as it sounds, it remains a form of manipulation. The fact that the adjustment sets up a reserve to be used in the future is seen by some as a more benign form of manipulation. But remember, if a company thinks it is acceptable to underreport revenues this year, it can use the same rationale to over-report revenues in the future. You deserve accurate reports, whether exceptionally optimistic or pessimistic; that is the only way you can truly judge a company.

6. *Reporting expenses early.* Just as higher-than-expected revenue can be sugar bowled to be used later, the same problem occurs when a company reports current year expenses in advance. And not only is the result the same, but the net income ratio also stays the same because both revenue and expenses are raised. A skilled CFO can make this happen and control the trend, at least for one or two years. The giveaway is found in the liability section as a "special charge" booked in the current year. So the journal entry increases expenses and sets up the special charge. When you see this odd credit next to liabilities and in the same year, both revenue and expense levels have grown considerably (but net profit percentage remains the same), it could mean that expenses have been booked early.

7. *Off-balance sheet subsidiaries.* This is a particularly troubling type of manipulation because it is difficult to find. Because a subsidiary is set

up off the balance sheet, it may be completely undisclosed or left to the fine print of the footnotes. Off-balance sheet subsidiaries can be used for all kinds of manipulation, and this technique was one of the favorite creative accounting methods used by Enron. For example, a company can loan money to its subsidiary and, without exchanging any funds, set up the obligation through journal entries. Then annual journal entries are made each year to report interest income by the parent company. Even though no cash has exchanged funds, this boosts net income through a series of sham transactions. A similar use of off-balance sheet subsidiaries is to assign some portion of current expenses to the subsidiary, which reports a large net loss. Meanwhile, the parent company can control the level of net earnings reported. It is completely false and misleading, but the results look spectacular.

8. *Converting reserves into income.* Companies set up reserves for many reasons. These include reserves for bad debts, which reduce the current asset value of accounts receivable, and reserves for absorption of merger and acquisition profit or loss. Companies carrying large credit-balance reserves can manipulate current year outcome by simply reclassifying all or part of the reserve balance to income. Explanations may be full of double-talk. For example: "Release of a portion of the deferred credit related to acquisition from the past period, to reflect accelerated marketing activity and to more accurately estimate the timing and recapture rate of the company's investment." Huh? Accounting explanations like these are popular, especially when manipulation has taken place.

9. *Extending the rate of write-offs to a longer time period.* Companies set up assets and amortize or depreciate them over a period of years. The intended purpose is to accurately report expenses or costs in the proper year. For example, a capital asset with a recovery period of 15 years is depreciated over 15 years, and if a company acquires another and agrees to a covenant not to compete, that asset (although intangible) may have a specified number of years of value. If a merger specifies this and the company agrees to the covenant for a five-year period, its assigned value may be set up as an asset and written off over five years. But net earnings are raised if and when the company decides to amortize an intangible asset over 10 years instead of over five. This is difficult to spot, because even the footnotes might not disclose the change. But watching the trend in amortization, you can spot the change and then start to ask questions.

10. *Odd changes in accounting policies.* Finally, companies can adjust reported net earnings simply by changing accounting policies. These tend to be quite complex and difficult to understand, but the details are going to be found in the footnotes. For example, a company may change the way it values inventory, which in turn could have a big effect on

calculation of the cost of goods sold and gross profit. If you see a sudden big change in gross profit, that is your red flag. But companies can also adopt different methods for recognizing revenues, meaning that they may book more income earlier (as long as this is rationalized in an accounting opinion somewhere in GAAP).

The key to finding manipulation is analysis. Here are some important suggestions:

1. *Always study the trend.* Eventually, all forms of manipulation are going to show up in an odd adjustment in the long-term trend, on the balance sheet, the income statement, or both.
2. *If it doesn't make sense, ask questions.* Call or e-mail a company's investor relations department to ask specific questions regarding footnotes, trends, or dubious changes in the financial statements.
3. *If explanations don't make sense, stay away.* None of this is so complicated that it cannot be explained in nonaccounting terms. Obfuscation is one of the unavoidable symptoms of manipulation.

The Bottom Line

- Stock prices over the long term move in the same direction as financial performance.
- The best performing stocks are those whose sales and income grow year after year.
- Companies with great stories and prospects may appear compelling, but unless the company delivers sales and profits, the long-term prospects for the stock will be poor.
- Companies' financial reporting might be manipulated to show improved short-term performance.
- It is important to review key financial metrics including revenues, earnings, cash flow from operations, and profit margin trends.
- All listed companies report on an accrual accounting basis. This makes each period's reported sales, costs, earnings, and net income accurate, but it also invites manipulation.
- Overstated revenue, changes in inventory valuation or capitalizing of general expenses are several ways companies can manipulate results.
- Watch cash flow by tracking both the current ratio and the debt ratio. If the current ratio is artificially maintained by transferring higher borrowings into current asset accounts, that is a red flag.

CHAPTER 5

Financial Projections
and Valuations

"Value criteria act like a chaperone at a party, making sure you don't fall for some sexy stock with a great story."
——James O'Shaughnessy, *What Works on Wall Street*

"Price is what you pay. Value is what you get."
——Warren Buffett

The goal of every investor is to accurately predict the future price movements of a given investment. With small-cap stocks, you need to be able, with some degree of accuracy, to make such predictions. Stocks often, but not always, move based on the underlying fundamentals of the company, primarily the current and historical financial performance and expectations for future results.

Financial performance is a key factor in share price movements, and it is the primary reason that some investments rise, while others fall. Over the short-term, news announcements may dictate the move in a stock's price, but every company that has achieved long-term, significant gains has done so by consistently reporting growth in earnings.

For this reason, the prediction of the future becomes the priority of the investor. Successfully predicting the future financial results for a company, and how those will line up with expectations, determines whether a stock will move higher or lower in the short-term.

Over the long-term, it is those companies that consistently grow their revenues, net income, and cash from operations that achieve year-after-year gains in their share price.

In some respects, analyzing past financial statements is the easy part. If the numbers appear good when looking in the rearview mirror, then the stock may be a good buy. However, there is a good reason that most investment prospectuses include text that reads, "Past performance is not indicative of future results." While performance in the recent past may be impressive, this doesn't mean it will be equally strong in the future. Past performance doesn't guarantee the future, but it should be considered a lagging indicator of the future. If performance hasn't been good in the past, I err on the side of caution and assume that the future won't be any better. A limited history of good results is far better than a long history of mediocre results.

I have explained how to evaluate a company as a prospective investment by determining if the management is qualified, the products are world-class, the sales strategy results in increasing sales, and the marketing is unique. Getting these important starting features identified is an essential first step.

Now you have to go to the next step: finding relevant financial trends and translating them into reliable forecasts. To some degree, you are going to depend on analysts to explain these to you; in other cases, you're better off developing your own analysis of trends and interpreting them. Remember, once forecasts are widely accepted and understood, it probably means the institutional investors have already taken positions and driven up the price. To get in early enough, you have to be able to estimate future growth trends before other investors come to the same conclusion.

Understanding Financial Guidance

A good starting point is to look at a company's internal financial projections about its financial future. The company and its management are a source of valuable information. No one knows better than management how likely it is that the company will be able to compete profitably, grow its markets, manage cash flow, and creatively approach the challenges of expansion. So to begin, think of the small cap's management as your first source of information.

Financial Guidance

A company's *financial guidance* is an estimate of upcoming operating results based on forecasting and budgeting within the company. It is intended to serve as a guide for investors, helping them to anticipate future results. Research analysts often use company guidance as a starting point for their own earnings estimates.

Some companies provide financial guidance, which is just as the name suggests—an early indication of future financial results. Public companies provide guidance to the public, including individuals, institutions, and analysts.

While management is biased, and often overly optimistic, they are also held accountable. Regularly promising great results and falling short is no way to build a happy base of shareholders, and managers know this. Failing to deliver on guidance often results in investors selling the stock due to their disappointment in the results. For this reason, managers aim to meet or exceed the guidance shared with the investing public.

Most public companies issue guidance at the time of the release of quarterly financial results, or through press releases updating guidance during the quarter. A company's website also has public relations with guidance.

The easiest way to see if a company has issued guidance is by checking one of the financial websites such as Yahoo! Finance or Google Finance. Simply enter the company's ticker or name and check the relevant new headlines or financial news reports that have been released. Financial guidance typically includes a few key metrics, including revenues, net income, and EPS. Other items that may be included are (EBITDA) and cash flow from operating activities. In the large-cap arena, a company's stock price will respond to new guidance almost immediately; with lesser known small caps there are far fewer people paying attention, and the information takes longer to circulate among investors, and therefore result in a move in share price.

A Reality Check

The next question, logically, is whether management's assessment of its growth potential is realistic. The art of forecasting consists of a series of educated guesses, and even when management makes its best effort to accurately judge growth trends, a number of reality checks get in the way, including:

1. *Making incorrect assumptions.* Anyone who has worked on a budget knows that its accuracy is going to rely on the underlying assumptions. The same is true when forecasting revenue and earnings growth. The company's management has to make its estimates based on realistic expectations about how well it can maintain growing revenue and earnings trends, how the competition will evolve, economic influences, and its own ability to set and realize goals. Even when looking only one quarter or one year into the future, accurate forecasting is a very elusive science, and no one can predict exactly what is going to happen even in the very short-term. Many companies provide guidance at the

time of the release of their financial results, either for the quarter or year. Guidance is typically updated to reflect the actual performance of the business. The best you can hope for is an educated guess based on known facts, including sales cycle and business pipeline.

For example, Cynosure (Nasdaq: CYNO) faced a potential loss in 2006 due to a legal dispute with Palomar Medical Technologies (Nasdaq: PMTI). Cynosure was accused of infringing on Palomar's licensed Anderson patents. However, the market overstated the maximum effect on future prices. If Cynosure's products had been found to infringe, it would have resulted in a one-time payment of $22.5 million plus 7.5 percent royalty expenses. In that event, the real impact on EPS would have been only one percent.

2. *Letting wishful thinking affect judgment.* As humans, we are all susceptible to hoping for the best in the future. This often affects the way that forecasting takes place. Remember, the future is "that period of time in which our affairs prosper, our friends are true, and our happiness is assured."[1]

For example, for Cynosure, analysts were way off in estimating earnings. For the fourth quarter of 2007, the company announced a loss of $2.5 million, or 19 cents per share, due to lower than expected revenues. In comparison, the company reported a profit of $5.3 million or 41 cents per share in the year ago quarter. Analysts polled by Thomson Reuters expected a loss of 7 cents per share on revenue of $25.4 million. "The global economic downturn has created an extremely challenging environment for the aesthetic industry," reported Cynosure President Michael Davin.

An idea of just how bad it really was can be seen by comparing the actual results reported with the analyst estimates (see Table 5.1).

3. *Assuming the current rate of growth will continue indefinitely.* One of the chronic problems in any forecasting is a simple calculation error. For example, if revenues and earnings have both been rising by 10 percent for the past three years, is it reasonable to assume they will rise by 10 percent next year? Most growth trends tend to begin leveling

TABLE 5.1   Actual Results vs. Analyst Estimates

Earnings History	Mar-08	Jun-08	Sep-08	Dec-08
EPS Est	0.38	0.46	0.45	−0.07
EPS Actual	0.45	0.46	0.37	−0.15
Difference	0.07	0.00	−0.08	−0.08
Surprise %	18.40	0.00	−17.80	−114.30

Source: Yahoo! Inc.

out as they extend into the future; so it makes sense to adjust future estimates to allow for this slow down in the future.

One example of a company with a very strong growth trend starting to level off is Panera Bread (NASDAQ: PNRA). This Richmond Heights, Missouri, company operates a chain of retail bakery cafés selling baked goods, soups, and salads. It was founded in 1981 as Au Bon Pain Co. and was re-launched in 1998 when it changed its name to Panera, to reflect the sale of many assets and a reorganization around the core Panera outlets. Panera was referred to as recession-proof. However, a look at its rate of growth over the decade ending in 2008 tells a different story. It looks like Panera recently moved into a significantly slower-growth mode.

For a number of years after its restructuring, Panera enjoyed revenue growth in excess of 30 percent. By 2006, that slowed to the high-20s (27.8 percent growth in 2006; 29.1 percent growth in 2007). Panera reported that total 2008 revenue grew 22 percent—a solid rate of growth in a year of recession, but a marked slowdown from growth rates just a few years earlier. And this slowdown came as the company continued to expand aggressively through new store openings.

4. *Placing emphasis exclusively on larger competitors.* A subtle problem is also found when management keeps an eye only on its larger competitors and ignores smaller companies coming up from the ranks. It is an easy mistake to make. The "big guy"—the leader in the sector with plenty of capital and most of the market share—is the most obvious competitive obstacle. But paying attention only to the larger rival means that management might not be thinking about smaller competitors as well. The assumptions about market share in the future often focus only on taking it away from larger companies, forgetting that smaller companies might also be taking a bite out of their share.

When the management team makes errors in spotting up-and-coming threats, it is costly. For example, in the late 1990s, Google (Nasdaq: GOOG) was still small enough to go under the radar while other search engines focused on larger competitors. At the time, there were a number of Internet search engines and larger Internet portals such as Yahoo, AOL, and MSN that incorporated search as part of their web sites.

By 1999–2000, investors were beginning to see more value in "pure search." However, it was not Google that most of them were focused on. At the time, the presumed leader was AltaVista, a spin-off of Compaq, which boasted a faster Web crawler than any of the competition and a bare-bones Web site that looked a lot like today's Google. But while Google more quietly worked on developing its technology, AltaVista took advantage of the hype of the day and went after larger competitors, such as Yahoo!, by touting its superior search engine as the company prepared to go public. Yet the AltaVista IPO was pulled at the last minute in 2000 due to the dot-com crash. And by the time the IPO market showed signs of stabilizing, Google's superior search engine had gained popularity had surged to the point that AltaVista was no longer relevant. These days, Google is a verb, and it's hard to remember a time that it was not a household name. But just a decade ago, it was not a household name. Google rose from relative obscurity very quickly. When was the last time you went to AltaVista.com to look for something?

Guidance Caveats

With these four common mistakes in mind, next evaluate what kind of guidance the company is providing. Is it aggressive, realistic, or conservative?

An *aggressive level of guidance* is found when the maximum level of good news is always assumed. There is no cushion or worst-case planning; in fact, forecasts may be exaggerated on the basic assumption that things will be likely to end up *better* than even an optimistic forecast. This is dangerous and misleading.

JA Solar Holdings, a Chinese solar cell manufacturer, had predicted strong growth for several periods. Then, in February 2009, JA lowered its 2009 revenue expectations, blaming global financial weakness and tightening credit markets as the cause. Share price fell 8.3 percent down 25 cents to $2.76 on this news. This was the consequence not only of market conditions, but also of aggressive guidance in previous periods and then a change to lowered expectations.

Realistic guidance assumes a mix of good and bad news, but it attempts to accurately estimate the outcome. This is what most people assume is always in play, but this just isn't necessarily the case. You need to compare past forecasts and outcomes to determine whether or not management is being realistic in its current forecasts.

Just as investors must aim to find companies led by executives who favor quality of earnings over quantity of earnings, we similarly must favor companies that utilize quality of guidance over quantity of guidance. Aggressive growth is rewarded by investors, while shortfalls are not tolerated.

A *conservative guidance* policy actually may understate the expectations for the coming year. There are two reasons for management to be conservative. First, this approach assumes that unknown events or competitive forces will reduce positive incomes. Second—and more disturbing—is the point of view that by being conservative, actual outcome will beat the estimate and will be seen as a positive earnings surprise. But by manufacturing this outcome with overly conservative guidance, management performs a disservice to would-be investors who seek accurate and reliable estimates.

Investors must seek out companies that have a history meeting or exceeding guidance. Guidance that isn't often met is worthless. For this reason, examining guidance and management's ability to accurately predict the future is required if investors are to put any faith in the quality of financial guidance.

Interpreting Analyst Estimates

If you focus solely on what analysts estimate for future earnings, you cannot expect to pick winning small caps. By the time analyst coverage is widespread, it is often too late to "beat the Street," and any run-up in value (not to mention a bargain price) has been quickly absorbed by other investors.

Projections Are Not Certain

Never assume that earnings or price targets are going to come true; like financial guidance, an analyst's projections are just that, projections. The information is valuable, but only when it is used with a range of other fundamental indicators and trends.

By paying attention to (1) reported and (2) final quarterly earnings, you can get a good idea of how much integrity goes into the numbers. A small cap is no different than a larger competitor in one respect: It is very difficult to make accurate quarterly or annual earnings estimates.

A great irony of analysts' estimates is the degree of importance given to them. In cases when an analyst predicts earnings and the actual comes in below that level, it is almost always treated as a negative. This is true even in situations when the company makes a separate earnings prediction and beats that prediction. Credence should be given to management and not so much to analysts, but the opposite is true. Investors tend to rely on analysts' forecasts, while often paying far less attention to the company's own reports.

For example, in February 2009, Moody's announced its current-year earnings guidance, which was below Wall Street analysts' expectations. Citing continued weakness in the markets, Moody's estimated EPS was between $1.40 and $1.50 for the year. In comparison, analysts polled by Thompson Reuters called for an EPS of $1.57. In a situation where the company's management has reduced guidance well below consensus analyst estimates, it is likely that the analysts will react and similarly lower their guidance. This reduction in guidance and estimates has the same effect as falling short of expectations: Shares often plunge.

Companies Play the Earnings Game

The forecasting of earnings and setting of price targets often is a self-defining game on Wall Street. While many analysts are skilled in corporate forecasting, many others simply ask a company's management for their estimates and then conform to these as forecasts. One danger to forecasting is that executives are capable of manufacturing the desired outcome to meet or exceed guidance and analyst expectations. Earlier in Chapter 4 I discussed GAAP accounting and signs to look for that might point to financial mismanagement.

For example, let's say a company has estimated that it is going to earn 53 cents per share over the next quarter and analysts all agree with this number. At the end of the quarter, actual reported earnings are 54 cents per share. This one-cent surprise causes the stock's price to rise the day of the earnings announcement. However, the company may have created this suspiciously close outcome with a simple journal entry. It may have consisted of any number of adjustments:

- Booking earned revenue early based on volume of current orders (actual and promised or verbally committed), but without booking the corresponding direct costs.
- Reducing the reserve for bad debts with the explanation that future bad debts are expected to be lower than previously estimated.
- Accelerating the positive write-off of reserves based on acquisition profits from a previous year's activity.
- Deferred expense payments *and* accruals, based on the false rationale that these expenses are not yet accrued.

All of these explanations sound good because they mimic legitimate and similar adjustments made by way of quarter-end accruals. But there is a problem with this kind of adjustment. The real intention is to meet earnings estimates or surpass them, to ensure investors and analysts that management is in control of growth, and also to make the case that its forecasting ability is quite good. The problems are even more serious. Consider, for example, the following:

■ Auditors may look at the books at the end of the quarter, but do not perform an in-depth analysis of transactions. The quarterly review is very preliminary and does not require the auditing firm to state specifically that the books look right. Only a glaring error is going to be revealed in this process.

■ The final accounting of the quarter often does not occur for several weeks after the end of the quarter itself. Thus, the earnings report is preliminary and can easily change later. But once the final accounting has been done and earnings are adjusted, investors have moved on, focused on the next quarter's estimate.

■ Even when last quarter's earnings are later changed, explanations are likely to be vague or nonexistent. They usually consist of downplaying the manipulation. But if investors do not pay attention to the interim-quarter shenanigans, they may miss an important truth: Many companies do *not* meet their quarter earnings estimates, even though their news releases say they do.

Financial Trends for Spotting Promising Small Caps

Earnings estimates invariably cover a period between three and 12 months. Anything going out beyond a year should be ignored, because no one knows with any certainty what the future holds. However, you can pick promising small-cap stocks by tracking results over the long-term.

Volatility

Volatility in year-to-year revenues and earnings often is a sign of unpredictable future growth. Ironically, with small caps, this might also be a symptom of a rapidly growing and dynamic company. The key to finding the difference is in whether or not subsequent adjustments are made and, ultimately, whether or not stock prices rise.

Financial trends you should follow to identify the most promising small-cap companies include:

1. *P/E.* The P/E ratio is the most embraced metric for valuing stocks. Simply put, it takes the share price divided by the earnings per share, generating a single number. A stock trading at $20 per share with EPS of $1 would have a PE of 20 ($20 divided by $1). Companies that

are considered more appealing are typically those with rapid growth, impressive profit margins, and a defendable competitive stance. These companies typically trade at higher PE ratios due to their desirability. PE is used to value companies based on their past or future earnings, and can help effectively determine whether a stock is over-valued, fairly valued, or under-valued relative to the stock market as a whole or its competitors.

As companies become larger, their growth rates often decline. And as the growth rate slows, the PE ratio typically declines. For this reason, it is important to find those select companies that are in the early stages of rapid growth and may be experiencing faster growth in the future, rather than slower growth.

2. *P/E to Growth.* P/E to Growth is also known as PEG. PEG calculates the P/E ratio of a stock in comparison to the growth rate. This calculation allows an investor to determine the valuation of the company relative to its growth rate. Since investors are buying a share in the future success of a business, using PEG to value a stock makes sense.

Once you've calculated P/E, deriving the PEG ratio is simple, and can be calculated on a historical basis using the previous year's numbers or those for a trailing 12-month period. Alternatively, you can use forward-looking metrics based on guidance or analyst estimates. Using an average of the growth rate for revenues and earnings, you can then quickly calculate PEG. A company with a P/E ratio of 20 and a growth rate of 30 percent would have a PEG of 0.66 (P/E of 20 divided by 30 percent growth rate).

When looking at PEG ratios, the lower the better, as this signifies growth at a reasonable price. A PEG ratio of one is usually accepted as fair value.

3. *Rate of growth.* A strong trend is always encouraging, especially when it comes to growing revenue and earnings. Growth in these numbers indicates that management has their eye on the prize and are affectively growing the business.

I define high-growth companies as those growing revenue and earning at over 20 percent. I've found that these companies are the ones that offer investors the biggest long-term potential for significant capital gains – the goal of small-cap investors. Finding companies with growth rates above 20 percent is not difficult, and the faster the rate of growth, the better. However, due consideration needs to be given to the valuation of the company. Buying growth stocks at any price is not the way to make consistent profits in small-cap stocks.

4. *Management compensation kept consistent over a growth period.* A responsible management policy is going to be to hold executive compensation steady during a period of initial growth. All too often, a small

company that is starting to grow experiences a period in which the founders cash in. They get themselves voted a handsome raise and bonus, basically taking new investor money out of the company to enrich themselves. If you see this taking place, get your money out *fast*, because it means management is not looking out for its shareholders. You should focus on companies whose management has pledged to keep its pay steady even as success starts to occur.

As long as management compensation is not raised to all-time levels while earnings are growing, you can have faith in the company. This is a sign that management really wants to grow the company and reward shareholders, rather than taking out as much as they can while the cash is available.

For example, Cell Therapeutics (Nasdaq: CTIC), a Seattle maker of lymphoma drugs, was ranked as the worst recession stock at the end of 2008. By Motley Fool's calculation, CEO James Bianco earned $1.58 for every dollar the company booked in revenues, a level of compensation way above a reasonable level for the circumstances. His published salary at the end of 2008 was $1.14 million. Cell Therapeutics is well ahead of Fool's second-worst recession stock, Biopure Corp., where CEO compensation worked out to $116,000 per million in revenue.

The point worth remembering about financial projections is that they are not always reliable. However, using some sound evaluation techniques, you can spot the reliable and reasonable estimates as well as the pie-in-the-sky, overly optimistic ones. Financial guidance relies on management's accuracy, and while many managers tend to be optimistic, they are going to be held accountable if their projections are too rosy.

Look out especially for incorrect assumptions, management's wishful thinking, claims that growth rates will continue indefinitely, and focus on larger competitors but not smaller ones. Also critically evaluate analysts' estimates to ensure that their forecasts are based on reliable trends. Notable among these trends are P/E range, revenue and earnings growth, and consistent management compensation.

The trend ultimately reveals everything, and even when some bad news gets hidden in a single year, it eventually gets revealed. When the books are being adjusted to make bad news look better, you will see:

- High volatility and unpredictability in reported revenues and earnings.
- Exceptionally high core earnings adjustments each year.
- Adjustments in each period for previously reported outcomes.
- Gyrations in P/E as well as EPS.
- Inconsistency in important capitalization ratios, notably the debt ratio (be especially concerned if the debt ratio increases every year).

The Bottom Line

- Stock prices move based upon financial results and expectations for future financial performance.
- Those companies that grow over time typically see their share prices increase accordingly.
- Financial guidance is a company's formal estimates of future financial results.
- Analyst estimates are the expectations of future financial results.
- Estimates are based on analysis of a researcher, taking into consideration financial guidance, industry trends, and other research.
- Growth at a reasonable price often yields outperforming stocks.
- Examining trends of performance can help to predict future results.

CHAPTER 6

Taking the Mystery Out of Technical Analysis and Trading for Quick Profits

"The trend is your friend."

—Anonymous

"Most of the time common stocks are subject to irrational and excessive price fluctuations in both directions as the consequence of the ingrained tendency of most people to speculate or gamble . . . to give way to hope, fear and greed."

—Benjamin Graham

Fundamentals are the focus of my successful approach to investing in small-cap stocks. Ultimately, it is the fundamentals that determine the long-term direction of a stock. But long-term growth and strong fundamentals alone don't assure successful investments. As with most things in life, timing is everything when it comes to investing. Fundamental research must be complimented by technical analysis, a useful tool for determining the ideal time for buying or selling a stock.

This chapter examines some of the basic technical theories and principles and shows how you can incorporate these into your program of analysis to find valuable small-cap stocks poised for gains in the near- and long-term.

In the time before the Internet, technical analysis was a cumbersome process because it demanded constant monitoring of a stock's price and volume, as well as calculation of moving averages and other metrics. Historically, technical analysis was not available to the average investor. However, technical analysis has been reborn due to automatic calculation of stock charts, multiple moving averages, instant calculation of even the most complex formulas, and—most important of all—simple and inexpensive *access* to streaming quotes. All of these are essential, and historical technical analysis looks ancient compared to what you can do today from your computer.

Many technical analysts, known as technicians, believe that price and volume are the whole story, that tracking price action anticipates and foretells the next price direction. There is a degree of truth to this belief, and I urge everyone to employ technical indicators. Technical analysis can become a self-fulfilling prophecy, with every trader examining the same charts, looking at the same movements and trends, and making the same trades as a result. This is the case now more than ever, with increasingly popular program trading by institutional investors. But rather than using technical analysis exclusively, I know a combination of fundamental and technical tests makes the most sense and yields the best returns.

Even if you are dedicated to the study of the fundamentals, a range of technical indicators is valuable. These indicators serve as a means for quantifying market risk, confirming what the fundamentals reveal, and signaling a change in the current trend.

As a starting point, remember the important distinction between the different kinds of analysis:

> *Fundamental analysis* focuses on analyzing the company's financial statements, management, competitiveness in the marketplace, and sector. Using this approach, the story of the company and the financial performance establish a comparative means for judging a company and its financial and competitive strength.
>
> *Technical analysis* focuses on the chart of a stock and the movements in share price. A technician looks for market strength or weakness based on current trends in the stock, chart patterns, and breakout signals.
>
> *Combined analysis* uses elements of both fundamental and technical schools. I like to combine many different trends and consider them valuable in different but equally important ways. It is also necessary to note that some key ratios, such as the P/E ratio, combine technical (price) with fundamentals (earnings) to track a stock.

A technician believes that price and volume are the whole story, that tracking price action anticipates and foretells the next price direction. There is a degree of truth to this belief, and I urge everyone to employ technical indicators.

Some Technical Basics

Everyone should be aware of some of the most basic price patterns that chartists and technicians look for. A premise of technical analysis is that specific patterns have meaning and tell you what the price is going to do next. If the price moves toward new upper or lower levels and breaks through, that often implies that a new trading range is being established, or that a new short-term trend is occurring and that prices are going to continue to move in the newly established direction. Equally important, if a price range test is made but fails, that often indicates that the price direction is now going to move in the opposite direction.

Trading Ranges

The first important technical indicator is called the trading range. This is the space between the highest and lowest price that a stock typically reaches within a period of time. As a company grows, the trading range, also known as the channel, will change as well, hopefully to the upside. The trading range defines volatility and also serves as the benchmark for most other indicators. For example, when a stock trades within a very narrow trading range, volatility is said to be low; meaning the market risk is lower. But risk has a flipside, called opportunity. So an exceptionally narrowly trading stock has both lower risk and lower opportunity.

Trading Range

The trading range defines a stock's volatility and market risk. The broader the range and the greater price movement within the range, the higher the volatility. When the barriers of the trading range are continually challenged and breached, the market risk (and profit or loss potential) is greatly increased as well.

The top of the trading range is called resistance, because it is known as the price limit within the current trading range. It is the highest price that buyers have recently paid. If resistance is ever passed, technicians see that as an indication that the price may rise further.

The bottom level is called support. This is the lowest price that a stock has sold at recently. If a stock's price falls below current support, it may signal a declining trend to a lower trading range.

In Figure 6.1, original resistance (1) is joined by two lower resistance levels (3, 5) and then lower again (6). When the price moved up from 4 the

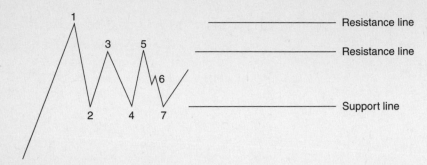

FIGURE 6.1   Example of Trading Range
Source: SmallCapInvestor.com

resistance level 3, would not allow prices to rise further. Initial support starts
at point 2 and the price tried twice to move lower than this point. Both times
the support level at point 2 held and prices moved higher. The more times a
price touches resistance or support points, the stronger the level of support
or resistance tends to be. If prices move beyond points 2 or 3 it is likely that
the asset will develop an entirely new trading range shortly afterwards.

Figure 6.2 shows a downward price channel until Jan 20. The stock
finally finds support at $50. For three weeks the stock struggles to move

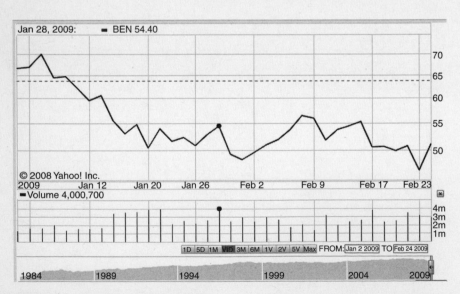

FIGURE 6.2   Example of Trading Range
Source: Yahoo! Inc.

higher. Each time $55 acts as resistance and $50 shows support. Finally, on Feb. 20 the support level breaks.

An important distinction has to be made between stationary and moving ranges. A stationary range remains level over time, and the moving range demonstrates an evolving price direction as seen in the above falling channel. Another way that trading ranges evolve is in the breadth itself. If a trading range of the recent past covered about six points but more recently has doubled to 12 points from high to low, that's a big increase in price volatility. If a stock's price range is trending upward but the breadth of the range remains the same, then the stock is not becoming more or less volatile. The same is true if price is trending to the downside; as long as the trading range's breadth is unchanged, that is a sign of no change in volatility or market risk. As you track stocks in growing small-cap companies, a growing price level with unchanged trading breadth is a very strong sign, indicating that future growth will continue to follow this trend.

For example, Range Resources (NYSE: RRC), a Fort Worth, Texas, independent oil and gas drilling company, was selling around $35 per share early in 2009, about half its all-time high of just over $76. However, between late 2002 and mid-2008 it showed a steady upward movement, marked by ups and downs on different days, which over time maintained a relatively narrow breadth.

Figure 6.3 shows an example of a rising prices without a change in breadth.

Note how the breadth of this evolving range holds the same range even as prices grow. Resistance and support both rise, but the breadth does not show any increase or decrease in volatility.

Figure 6.4 is somewhat different. The breadth remains the same as the price trend increases; the *breakdown* occurs once price moves below support. This is an important signal, especially after a long-established upward

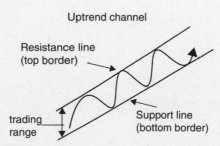

FIGURE 6.3   Example of the Uptrend "Channel"
Source: SmallCapInvestor.com

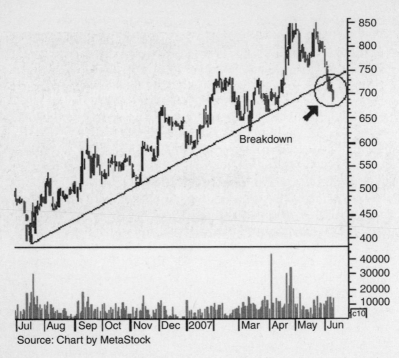

Source: Chart by MetaStock

FIGURE 6.4 Example of the "Breakdown"
Source: MetaStock

trend. A breakdown means that the share price has collapsed, falling below the support level. This can indicate lower prices in the future.

Figure 6.5 shows a long-term trading range. Prices gradually increase over time in a relatively low-volume trading range. However, in April, it looks like the range is beginning to grow in volatility. For the technician, this sudden burst in prices could signal an improvement in the price trend, depending on whether that is confirmed by other technical indicators such as MACD and RSI. If it is not, then the technician would expect this strong rise in price to be followed by a retreat back to previously established levels.

The same observation works on the way down. Figure 6.6 shows a declining price trend without any change in breadth. The breakout to the upside would be confirmed by the analysis of other technicial indicators, notably changes in daily volume.

With the trading range serving as the basis for most technical analysis, and resistance and support serving as the lines in the sand for significant price movement, there are six important technical patterns you need to know:

FIGURE 6.5 Example of a Long-Term Trading Range
Source: QuoteMedia

1. *Double tops or bottoms.* In this very common pattern, price trends move toward a top or bottom. In a double top, it is likely that the price will spike close to resistance, retreat, and then spike once again. When price double tops like this without successfully breaking through resistance, technicians believe it foreshadows a *decline* in price. So the pattern following the double top is for prices to move downward. In a double

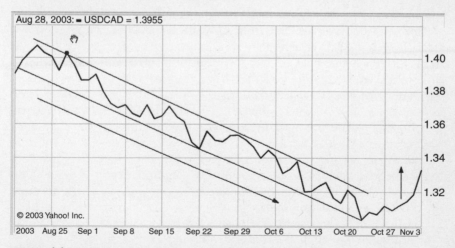

FIGURE 6.6 Example of the Downtrend "Channel"
Source: Yahoo! Inc.

FIGURE 6.7   Example of a Double Top

Source: Yahoo! Inc.

bottom, the opposite occurs. Price trends down to support and spikes twice, only to retreat. This anticipates a rise in price after the double bottom.

Here's an example of a double top: Questcor Pharmaceuticals (Nasdaq: QCOR) experienced a double top between December 2008 and January 2009. This is shown in Figure 6.7. As the pattern often foreshadows, the double top was followed by a sharp decline in price.

Double tops and bottoms are very common patterns. They are easy to spot and interpret. However, as with all patterns, a double top or bottom can also be misread. False indicators do occur, so it helps to have some experience in chart interpretation and a working knowledge about a company's fundamentals.

2. *Head and shoulders.* Similar to double tops and double bottoms is an equally important pattern: the head and shoulders. In this chart pattern, price spikes upward in three parts. The first and third are the shoulders, and the second is the head. The head spike is higher than the two shoulders and often reaches right to the level of resistance. Following the head and shoulders pattern without continuing upward, prices tend to fall. This is a reliable formation that leads to further decline. Also, the total decline is usually the twice the difference between the neckline and the top of the head. See Figure 6.8 for a diagram of this pattern, and Figure 6.9 for an actual stock trend in this pattern.

A reverse head and shoulders displays the same pattern, but on the downside and at support. It consists of three downward price spikes,

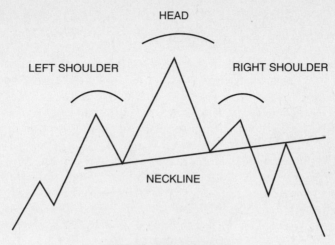

HEAD AND SHOULDERS
AS A REVERSAL PATTERN IN AN UPTREND
(BEARISH)

FIGURE 6.8   Diagram of Head and Shoulders Pattern

Source: SmallCapInvestor.com

FIGURE 6.9   Stock Trend of Head and Shoulders Pattern

Source: Chart Patterns

with the middle one (the head) moving lower than the first and third (shoulders). It precedes a price increase. Figure 6.10 shows the reverse head and shoulders.

3. *Triangles.* The triangle is most often a continuation pattern, which means it confirms the current trend and gives a signal that price is going to move in the same direction. Some very specific triangle patterns can also be *reversal* signals, which mean the current trend is slowing down and price levels may turn in the opposite direction in the near future.

The three triangle patterns are ascending, descending, and symmetrical. Triangles generally start out with their widest trading range and then narrow. An ascending triangle is characterized by a narrowing trading range with price levels finishing on the higher side of the range, or even culminating in a breakout above previously established resistance. This is a bullish pattern for the stock as depicted in figure 6.11.

After moving higher following an uptrend, the price of the stock reaches a wall of resistance. Each time the price moves up to the resistance point it quickly moves lower. Buyers are still interested in the stock, so each downward move is met with buying. As a result, each pullback brings less downward movement. Finally, the buyers overwhelm the stock and the price quickly moves beyond the former resistance level.

A descending triangle ends up with the narrowest portion ending on the lower side—near support—or even breaking out beneath it. This is a bearish signal and, just as the ascending implies a continuing upward trend, the descending implies that the downward trend is going to continue.

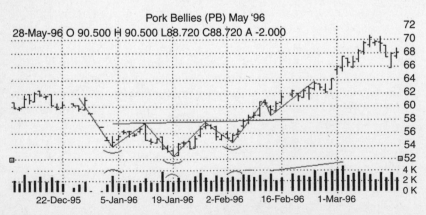

FIGURE 6.10   Diagram of Reverse Head and Shoulders Pattern

Source: Chart Patterns

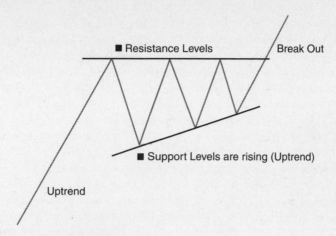

FIGURE 6.11 Ascending Triangle Chart
Source: AboutCurrency.com

The symmetrical triangle implies that price is in a period of consolidation, and no one is sure where it is going to move next. Volume may also be low in these situations, leading to a narrowing of the trading range and overall uncertainty. Most traders will want to wait out this pattern until something more specific emerges.

4. *Flags and pennants.* The patterns known as flags and pennants are similar to triangles in the sense that the patterns are created by changes in the trading range's breadth. They are both considered as continuation patterns and are most often seen when price levels are consolidating. The two terms—flags and pennants—are often used to mean the same pattern. However, a flag is likely to be found in a rectangle, and a pennant is shaped more like a triangle.

The flag is characterized by a significant price movement and then a sideways pattern. It concludes most often with a price breakout (above resistance for upside continuation, or below support for downside price trends). The initial price spike is called the flag pole, and the horizontal trend is the flag itself. Descriptions of flags as continuation patterns are very helpful in understanding the meaning of the pattern. For example, once the horizontal movement begins, technicians believe the flag is flying at half-mast, anticipating the subsequent price movement to continue the trend. In other words, the half-mast time is a consolidation in the middle of the trend. The distinction between flags and pennants is found in the breath of the trading range. In the flag, the overall trend may be evolving upward or downward, but the breadth remains the same (thus the rectangular shape). Once price levels break above resistance, a buy signal is normally triggered, or in a downtrend, once price falls below support, a sell signal is triggered.

As seen in Figure 6.12, in 2007 the GLD, which tracks the price movement of gold, formed two bull flag patterns. Both times the patterns played out perfectly. The result were huge gains for any investor who bough GLD during the flag formation.

The pennant shares all of the flag's attributes with one important distinction: The trading range changes over time, often further characterized by a series of tests of resistance (in uptrends) or support (in downtrends) and possibly also signaling a reversal if and when double tops or bottoms occur as part of a pennant pattern.

The shape of the flag or pennant depicts bullish or bearish trends (see Figure 6.13). Note how the pattern occurs in the middle of an established direction in all cases; these flags and pennants are pauses for consolidation before the established trends resume.

5. *Wedges.* The wedge often signals a reversal in the current trend. The wedge is similar to the triangle, but tends to take much longer to develop. The wedge term could be as long as several months. It demonstrates a convergence of resistance and support over this period, while overall price levels trend upward or downward. So the wedge contains a narrowing trading range while signaling price direction change. In a falling wedge, the sentiment is bullish because you would anticipate a price reversal to the upside at the end of the wedge. The slope of the top, or resistance, is probably going to be sharper than the slope of the descending support line, which may even be flat. Within the wedge, expect to see at least two tests of both resistance and support. These double tops and bottoms are part of the wedge development. A buy signal occurs when the price finally breaks through resistance and begins moving upward. This normally is also accompanied by heavier than normal volume.

The rising wedge is exactly the opposite. It demonstrates an ascending and narrowing price range. It is bearish, and you should expect price tests on the top and the bottom, culminating in a breakout below support. This is a sell signal at the conclusion of the wedge.

6. *Gaps.* Any time a space is found between one period's closing price and the next period's opening price, a gap has been formed. A "period" is normally a single trading day, but some traders (notably day traders and micro traders) also track 15-minute or 5-minute charts, looking for important signals. One important attribute of chart patterns is that all of the generally observed significance to patterns apply whether in very fast charting or over extended periods of time. In Figure 6.14, note the narrowing trading range in the form of a pennant, ending with an important combination of an upward price gap *and* a following strong breakout to the upside.

There are many different kinds of gaps. A *common gap* is found in any stock with even moderate volatility and does not really signal

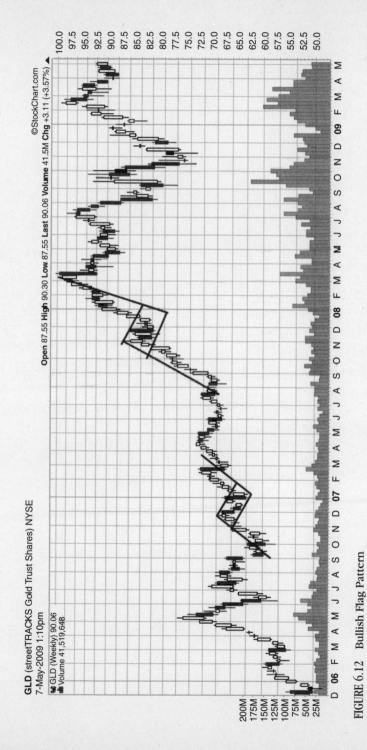

FIGURE 6.12   Bullish Flag Pattern

Source: Chart courtesy of StockCharts.com

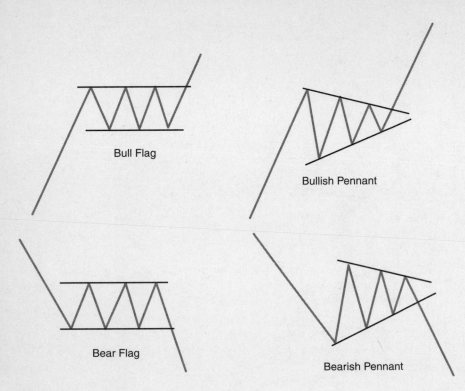

FIGURE 6.13 Bullish or Bearish Flags or Pennants
Source: SmallCapInvestor.com

FIGURE 6.14 Gaps in a Stock Chart
Source: Yahoo! Inc.

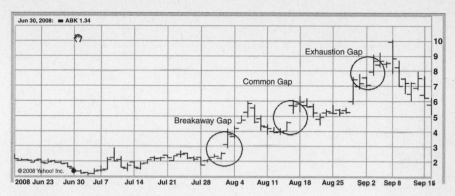

FIGURE 6.15   Three Types of Gaps
Source: Yahoo! Inc.

any changes in the current trend. But *runaway* and *breakout* gaps are very meaningful. A runaway gap involves a series of gaps, one after the other and in the same price direction. A breakaway gap occurs when the gap itself moves price through resistance or support. These gaps generally are the start of a major price movement. As the short-term trend begins to end, an *exhaustion* gap is likely to occur, which is either accompanied by or shortly followed by high volume. This normally signals that prices are going to stop moving in the current direction and move in the opposite direction. These are generalizations, but they can be useful for confirming trends noticed by other signals, such as double tops or bottoms, head-and-shoulders patterns, and changes in volume.

Figure 6.15 shows three the types of gaps, which often will be seen as part of a short-term trend within a short period of time.

Entry and Exit Signals

Technicians also like to look for entry and exit signals, and they use a variety of patterns to perfect their timing. There are many of these, but the most effective entry and exit patterns are those combining two or three different trends. For example, a three-part signal (to sell at the top of an uptrend or to buy at the bottom of a downtrend) may involve three signals occurring together:

1. *Three or more periods of uptrend or downtrend movement.* By definition, the uptrend has to include periods of high prices above the previous day *and* low prices above the previous day. And downtrend patterns have to include periods with lower lows and lower highs. If you use

A Candlestick Chart

A candlestick chart summarizes daily information with a rectangle and extending points above and below. A black or other-colored rectangle appears when the day's price moves down; a white or clear rectangle means prices moved up. The top edge of the rectangle is the closing price (on a clear box) or opening price (on a black box); the reverse is true for the bottom edge of the rectangle. The extent of the extensions above and below the rectangle represents the range of trading for the day. Candlesticks are valuable and are used by technicians because of their visual representation of trends over a period of time.

candlestick charts, these are easy to spot. The trading range of each period clearly rises above or falls below the prior period in three or more periods.

2. *A narrow-range day (NRD).* This is a day (or other period) in which the range of price between high and low are exceptionally small or even flat. This may signal the end of the trend established in step one.

3. *Exceptionally high volume.* When volume levels spike at the same time (or within one session) of indicators 1 and 2 above, it is a very strong confirmation that the existing trend has come to an end and that prices are about to move in the opposite direction.

The three-part entry/exit approach (three or more periods in the same direction, a narrow-range day, and high volume) is used by day traders and swing traders to time entry (at the bottom) and exit (at the top). The three trends not only confirm one another but enable you to hold off making entry or exit too early. For example, the trading range trend requires at least three periods, but it could go on for many more periods. So how do you know when to make your move? The answer is to seek all three signals together. When they occur, they cross-confirm and set up a very consistent and useful signal.

Accumulation and Distribution

The concepts of accumulation and distribution explain how and why price trends are established and evolve. The trend in supply and demand for shares of stock works as a momentum indicator. If investors are accumulating (buying) or distributing (selling), you can identify divergences between the current stock price and volume. The formula for calculating Accumulation and Distribution (A/D) is:

$$\left(\text{close} - \text{low}\right) - \left(\text{high} - \text{close}\right) \div \left(\text{close} - \text{low}\right) \times \text{volume} = \text{A/D}$$

This single-value indicator is tracked over a period of days to spot emerging trends in the supply and demand for shares. So a period of upward-trending days with high volume, which takes place in a longer-period downtrend, may imply that demand for shares is starting to increase. This would mean price pressure will emerge, moving the price trend higher. Or if a series of downtrend days with higher-than-average volume is seen in an otherwise upward-trending period, it indicates that price levels are weakening for those shares. The emerging A/D trend should be confirmed by other indicators (testing patterns, narrow-range days, etc.) before trading action is initiated.

The concepts of convergence and divergence act in concert with accumulation and distribution to anticipate new price trends. Convergence is the movement of price toward the current moving average, and divergence is the movement of price away from a moving average of prices. The trends in convergence and divergence of price, studied in conjunction with accumulation and distribution, provide good indication of the price or weakness in the current trend, or likely future movements toward or away from averages, and strength or weakness in the current price levels.

Convergence and divergence are based on comparative analysis between price and moving averages. Many different moving averages can be used in this analysis, and the use of two or more at the same time makes analysis more revealing as well. You want to look for crossover points, where the price and moving average meet and then move apart. As a general observation, when the moving average is lower than current price levels that is a sign of price strength, and when current price levels are below the moving average, that is a sign of weakness. It's all about averages and the strength or weakness of price as it is viewed today. The smoothing effect of moving averages helps to better understand the strength or weakness of price when the two are viewed together.

An effective application of this theory is known as moving average convergence/divergence, or MACD. This is called a dynamic indicator because it applies the significance of two moving averages to current price. It employs calculation of the difference between a 26-period and a 12-period exponential moving average (EMA) to find signal lines and plot them on a MACD chart.

This analytical tool is most effective for stocks with high volatility. You can identify three kinds of signals in current stock prices using MACD: Crossover points, overbought or oversold conditions, and divergences.

Techniques other than the 26/12 averages are used in some cases, with adjustments based on volatility levels of a particular stock.

The crossover is important because it signals a change in current conditions. So as price moves either above or below the MACD line, technicians take that as a sign that sentiment has flipped. The indicator also tells when a stock is overbought or oversold, because the MACD line diverges further from price on the upside (oversold) or on the downside (overbought). The level of divergence can be interpreted in a number of ways, so that MACD is often used not as a primary indicator, but to confirm other technical signs.

The Relative Price of a Stock

Closely related to the emerging strength or weakness of price is an indicator called *relative price*. This is a measure of the price trends in relation to the trends in other stocks in the same industry or against the broader market. The relative strength indicator (RSI) measures this trend. This is a technical momentum indicator that quantifies the magnitude of gains and losses to determine whether the stock is overbought or oversold.

The formula for relative price strength begins by dividing the current price by the index. Tracking this relationship using each day's closing price, you can gauge whether the stock is performing better or worse than the market as each value climbs. As the stock and index fall, a stronger stock will fall at a slower rate than the index. So relative price strength is useful only when the relative trend is observed over a period of time. The appeal of this barometer is that it enables you to apply a simple formula to draw a meaningful conclusion about the price strength of a single stock. A key momentum indicator, the trend of relative price strength is used to time entry and exit decisions based on improving or deteriorating levels. For example, a stock that has underperformed the S&P500 for a long time may begin to show signs of strengthening. Momentum investors may see this change as an early sign that the stock is going to outperform the market in the future. The same observation works when you have bought shares in a company whose stock has outperformed the market for many months. When is the right time to sell? Momentum traders look for signs of a drop in relative price strength to signal an exit. Using the relative price strength trend helps to time entry and exit for stocks as well as for tracking the emergence of different supply and demand factors; these are often subtle, so relative price strength, even though backward-tracking, remains an important technical indicator. It may signal a change before most other technical signs, or it can be applied to verify that a stock's continuing strength has not changed.

Another advantage to using relative price strength is that it can be calculated over any time period. Very short-term traders may track relative price strength over a limited number of days, and traders willing to wait for longer time periods, who are more able to hold a promising stock as long as it remains successful, may want to use relative price strength over several months.

The key change in relative price strength, represented by strengthening or weakening trend lines or even crossover points, is believed by many technicians to anticipate more specific signals like breakouts and strong price reversals. Relative price strength, accompanied by observation of changes in the patterns of trading ranges and resistance or support tests, can serve as an important early indicator of new trends in a stock's price.

All technical indicators are generalizations, and none by themselves can be used reliably to make specific trading decisions. But used in groupings, technical indicators are effective tools for timing of entry and exit. In addition, technical indicators can be used to confirm emerging fundamental trends in a company's ever-changing competitive stance. The best approach to studying a company is utilizing a wise combination of fundamental and technical indicators, and tracking both types over a period of time.

The Bottom Line

- Technical analysis can compliment fundamental research, helping determine the timing of trades to maximize profits.
- Institutional investors can use technical analysis for program trading based on the technical movements of stocks.
- Stocks trade within ranges, and when those ranges are violated, share prices are likely to move either higher or lower, depending on the direction of the movement.
- Institutional investors are responsible for most trading volume.
- Breakouts on heavy volume are a better indication of the direction than those that occur on low share volume.
- Technical analysis can be effectively used to determine the short-term direction of a stock.
- Long-term, stocks move based on the fundamentals, not based on the technicals.

CHAPTER 7

Trading Strategies for Successfully Buying and Selling Small-Cap Stocks

"The individual investor should act consistently as an investor and not as a speculator. This means...that he should be able to justify every purchase he makes and each price he pays by impersonal, objective reasoning that satisfies him that he is getting more than his money's worth for his purchase."

—Benjamin Graham

Picking great small-cap companies with lots of promise, strong financial performance, and attractive valuations is the starting point to profitable investing. You want to make sure that you increase the odds of success and focus on those small caps with the greatest potential for dazzling returns and growth. This requires not only smart analysis of the facts, but also a keen sense of timing. As with most things in life, timing is everything. You can increase potential profits by timing your entry *and* exit skillfully.

This chapter gives you the tools to protect your positions in small-cap stocks and to counter the effects of volatility if the price does fall below your purchase price. I cover issues important to every investor such as the details of different kinds of orders and an analysis of the many risks you face. Everyone needs to evaluate their ever-changing risk tolerance with many considerations in mind: age, experience, income and tax situation, and long-term personal goals. These are not complex issues, but sadly, they often are not addressed by investors. Investors must ask themselves (1) how much risk is appropriate, (2) what is my financial goal, and (3) how to weigh the risks investments to find appropriate methods for accomplishing those goals.

Liquidity Considerations with Small-Cap Investing

Liquidity refers to the ability of investors to get into and out of their investments. Those stocks that have many shareholders and trade frequently with large share volume are considered liquid—it is easy to find a buyer or seller. Those stocks with few shareholders, infrequent trading, and low share volume are deemed illiquid.

Most small-cap stocks fall into the latter category, and are considered to be illiquid stocks. The reason is that the companies are smaller—meaning there are fewer shares issued, and likewise fewer shareholders including individual investors, institutions, and traders. This means that there are less people buying and selling shares of small caps compared with mid- and large-cap stocks. For example, Graham Corp. (AMEX: GHM), a small cap with a market cap of $89 million that I discussed in Chapter 3, has only 10 million shares outstanding. Google (Nasdaq: GOOG) on the other hand has a $100 billion market cap and 240 million shares outstanding.

It's no surprise that with a larger number of shares outstanding and a larger market cap, and Google has more frequent trading in its stock. Most financial web sites report a statistic called Average Share Volume, which represents the average number of shares traded per day over the trailing three months. Graham trades an average of 181,000 shares a day valued at less than $2 million. Meanwhile, Google trades an average of 5.5 million shares a day, valued at roughly $2 billion. Clearly, it is easier to find a buyer or seller for Google than Graham, simply due to the higher share volume. Greater share volume and liquidity makes for a more efficient market for buying and selling a stock. Small-cap stocks are often not as liquid as larger stocks. As a result, it can be difficult to buy and sell shares at attractive prices, and the share price at times doesn't represent the true value of the company.

Liquidity

Illiquidity and Volatility Liquidity for small caps is nothing like liquidity for widely held large-cap issues. Not only is trading volume going to be much lower, but small caps also do not always enjoy an efficient market simply because the numbers of shares outstanding is quite small.

Due to the illiquidity of many small-cap stocks, the share prices also tend to be more volatile. This means that the share prices tend to rise and fall more rapidly, since the market is less efficient due to fewer shares trading hands and fewer investors buying and selling. Prices of many small caps move quickly on news or speculation, and can make buying and selling challenging.

Order Types for Trading Small Caps

Once you've identified the right investment, there are many ways to place an order to buy or sell a stock. While these order types can be used for any type of stock, there are benefits of each trade that are specific to small cap investments. Here is a summary of the various types of orders that can be used for placing trades:

1. *Market order.* The standard, default order is called a market order. This simply means that your trade will be executed at the current market price. Market orders are generally executed immediately at the best price offered by a market maker, a firm that is quoting a buy a sell price for stock. The market maker is required to offer shares for purchase and sale at a price of its choosing. For investors buying large blocks of shares, it is important to note that a market maker guarantees to buy or sell only a certain number of shares at a set price (this could be anywhere between 100 and over 5,000 shares). A market order to buy or sell is an instruction to your broker to transact at the prevailing price at the time of execution. For small caps with low volatility, the market order is an easy one to place. However, with more volatile stocks, you might get some unexpected surprises upon execution. Use market orders if you must buy or sell a stock immediately and the execution of the trade is more important to you than the price of the transaction. This can be important when you're trying to buy a stock that is running higher and are confident that you need to own the stock, even if the trade execution may be at a higher price. Likewise, if a stock is falling quickly due to bad news, use of a market sell order to exit a position can be prudent.

   In most circumstances, using market orders is not advisable, since the price of a small-cap stock tends to be more volatile than their large-cap cousins, due to lowered liquidity and greater volatility. Instead, I recommend using limit orders (see below) to narrow down the specific trade you would like, and at an exact price. While these trades don't get executed as quickly as a market order, you'll have the assurance that the trade will be made at your desired price (if it is executed).

2. *Stop loss.* As the name suggests, the stop-loss order is used to limit losses. This order includes a price trigger that generates a sell if the stock falls to a specified price level. When shares fall to the prescribed price, a market order to sell the stock is executed. This may mean that the trade is executed at the stop-loss price, or below that price in a fast moving market. This is a wise form of protection when you are in a highly volatile market, and especially if the market risk and volatility levels for your stock are higher than average. You pick the stop-loss price knowing that the stock is going to be sold when that price is

triggered. This order is best used to protect downside exposure by limiting potential losses from your stocks. With small caps, you must be careful, as the volatility could "stop out" a position based on intra-day volatility. Therefore, use these cautiously, and set them at a price at which you'll definitely want to sell the stock. For hands-on investors watching the market, stop losses are less useful, since you're always watching your positions.

3. *Trailing stops.* A useful variation on the stop-loss order is the trailing stop. In this situation, you are preserving paper profits rather than limiting losses. In cases where your small-cap stock has appreciated, a trailing stop is a smart order to have in place. The order represents a fixed percentage of the current market price. If the price falls by that percentage or more, the trailing stop becomes a market order and a sell is placed. But if the stock's price continues on its upward rise, the trailing stop continues in force without any action. It only goes into effect if the price falls from a high point to the percentage set in your standing order. Like the risks of a stop loss, this can cause problems for small-cap investors. If a stock rises quickly, and then falls back from a high price, the shares would be sold using a trailing stop. The concern here is that your broker could automatically sell a stock you wish to continue owning.

4. *Limit orders.* When you place a limit order, you state the exact price at which you want to make a purchase or sale. The order will only be placed if that price is available. This is a smart way to buy and sell small caps, because you set and control the price; if the market price varies from that level, the buy or sell order will not go through. However, limit orders are not effective if you want to make the trade *immediately*, since the trade may not be executed.

5. *At or better.* This is a variation on limit orders. In the usual limit order, the trade is triggered once the specified price is reached, even though the actual trade value may be higher or lower. This varies by brokers' definitions of the limit itself. Some traders use at or better as part of the order. Thus, a buy order will be executed at or below the limit price, and sell orders will be executed at or above the limit price.

6. *All or none.* This order qualifies another type of order and is often used in combination orders. These are orders involving both stock and option positions such as spreads, straddles, or covered calls. A spread is the opening of two or more positions with exercise or strike prices both above and below the current stock price. A straddle also involves two or more positions, but at identical expiration prices. A covered call is the sale of a call option when the seller also owns 100 shares of the underlying stock. It tells your broker that all of the indicated positions have to be executed at the same time, or if that is not possible, none

of the components in the order should be executed. This is crucial when positions hedge risks; opening only part of the overall combined position would consequently expose the trader to unwanted risk levels. Small-cap investors might find themselves using an all or none order in some cases. For example, you might want to hedge a long small-cap position against a short position in an index, ETF or option. This order is used primarily by very advanced traders and speculators.

7. *Good till canceled*. This is a special type of order that remains open until it is either executed or you cancel it. The good till canceled order can be applied to any other form of order, although your broker might place a limit on the duration you are allowed to keep the trade open. This order is good for some small-cap situations. For example, if you are tracking a stock and thinking of entering a position at a particular price, a good till cancelled order programs your specifications and keeps the order on the books unless you change your mind and cancel it later. A good till cancelled order on the sell side can be used in conjunction with the stop loss with an indefinite timeframe.

8. *Day order*. Every order except the good till cancelled order is treated as a day order automatically. This means that an order you place today is going to either be executed during the current session or will expire. If you want it to continue, it has to be re-entered the next day.

9. *On close or on open*. You can also set a specific time when you want your order to be executed. In some scenarios, you might want to enter your small-cap trade at the close of business. In other cases, you can enter an after-hours order to be executed "on open," meaning the order will be executed as soon as the stock market opens the following day. This variation to an order is often used by day traders.

All of the order variations are designed to enable you to control the actual price points for your trades. These are especially valuable in small-cap investing, considering the problems of liquidity in a limited market with a limited number of shares available.

Risk Tolerance

The liquidity issues associated with small-cap investing are unavoidable. However, these are manageable through application of the right order formats, diversification (see Chapter 8), proper timing of decisions, and averaging techniques. A more immediate concern is the market risk itself, most often seen in the form of price volatility.

If investors have a single complaint or concern about small caps, it inevitably relates to the volatility of these stocks and their perceived risk.

Dealing with this price volatility is equally as challenging as picking the right stock. Stop-loss and trailing stop orders can only go so far in protecting you against the market conditions so often experienced in high-volatility small-cap stocks. You have to ensure that the selections you make are appropriate matches for your personal risk-tolerance level.

Making It Personal

Personal risk tolerance is different for everyone and far more complicated than the common belief that all investors are the same: They want profits but not losses. On examination, you quickly realize that risk tolerance is more complex, and just as important, it changes as your investment exposure, age, income, and experience all evolve.

Risk tolerance is going to vary based on many factors, and no two people are going to be identical in how they define this for themselves. These factors include:

1. *Age.* Most people understand that the longer the time to retirement, the more risks they can *afford* to take, and the shorter that time, the more they need to preserve capital. Although these generalizations are true, your age has more to do with risk than just counting the number of years to retirement. And incidentally, the concept of retirement as a period when your income just stops is not universally true, so here again, everyone will define this in his or her own way. You also will want to consider your priorities, based on your age. For example, you might be looking forward to eventually breaking out of the corporate grind and starting your own business; if you are planning for this, you might have a target date in mind, and this certainly affects the level and degree of risk you are willing to take.
2. *Income and assets.* Your current level of income and assets directly influences risk as well. If you have adequate income to put aside a sizeable dollar amount each month to invest (the level of what is cynically called "disposable" income), then you are naturally going to be able to live with greater risks than others. Some people barely get by on their income and cannot afford *any* risk. Your assets also play a part. If you have considerable assets, this affects how you look at risk. If you own a home and have a mortgage, the cash flow including that mortgage payment affects risk; if you own your home free and clear, the investment possibilities are greater and your risk horizon can expand as well.

3. *Experience and knowledge.* The degree of your own experience and knowledge is very important in deciding your appropriate level of risk tolerance. The greater your experience, the better you comprehend the direct relationship between risk and profit potential, and the greater your knowledge as an investor, the less fearful you are of otherwise unknown risks. These two working together—experience and knowledge—define how risk tolerance is going to evolve as your exposure changes, income and assets grow, and your life situation changes over time. The past experience of each investor also impacts that outlook and risk tolerance. For example, investors who have survived a bear market and experienced a recovery in the stock market are likely to be more tolerant the next time stocks head lower. While those inexperienced investors who have never been through the bad times are more likely to throw in the towel when the going gets tough.

4. *Investing venue.* You may invest differently in your personal accounts than you do in your IRA or other retirement plan. You may also adopt different risk postures when buying stocks directly versus buying shares in a mutual fund. This is true even when some stocks have lower market risk than some mutual funds. It is wise to understand how the venue affects your attitude toward risk, and how this reality might distort your perception of risk tolerance.

5. *Tax situation.* If your income is higher than average, your income tax burden is always on your mind when you invest. The tendency is to seek investments with tax-deferral provisions, to defer selling profitable positions until the following year, and even to seek investments with less potential just to keep the tax burden down. The tax burden is aggravated when you are subject not only to federal taxes, but also to high state taxes or even a municipal income tax. Be aware of how positioning yourself as a small-cap investor will affect your tax liabilities, but don't allow tax considerations to affect how you otherwise make risk evaluations, pick stocks, and time your buy and sell decisions.

6. *Family situation.* Your family situation also affects the degree of risk you are willing and able to assume. A young, single professional with plenty of income, no mortgage payment, and many years before even thinking about retirement will probably have a vastly different risk-tolerance level than a married investor with a spouse, children, mortgage, and car payments, who has no immediate prospects to free up disposable income during the next few years.

7. *Major life events.* I know that all of us have to change our risk profile based on the major changes in our lives. These include graduating from college, landing the first job, getting married, buying a home, having a child, paying off a mortgage, starting your own business, paying for a child's college education, and retiring. All of these are positives. On the

negative side, life events can include bankruptcy, divorce, loss of a job, poor health, and the death of a loved one. Some of these events can be mitigated through insurance, while others are unavoidable and cannot be planned for, but when they occur, they certainly change your risk profile in significant ways.

Risk Awareness, an Essential Attribute

How many different kinds of risk do you face as an investor? Some people are surprised to discover that, in fact, there are many different kinds of risk, and we all face them. It is easy to simplify risk in your mind, to assume that either there is only one kind of risk (prices will fall instead of rise) or that risk doesn't really matter if you do your homework. Neither of these is really true; risk is the flip side of opportunity, and it comes in many types. These include:

1. *Market risk.* The best-known risk of all is market risk. There is a general assumption, especially among new or inexperienced investors, that the purchase price of a stock is the "zero" or base, the starting point. It is important to remember the basic reality of market risk: Prices can rise or fall. For example, iCAD Inc. (Nasdaq: ICAD), which makes equipment to detect breast cancer, was rising rapidly early in 2008, moving from $2.14 up to $4.60 after the FDA approved broader uses for its products. But in spite of the good news, the weak market took its toll. By early 2009, iCAD was trading at only 89 cents per share.

    Whenever you invest in a stock, it's important to evaluate the pros and cons based on the fundamentals and all of the attributes I have explained in previous chapters. But it is also important to evaluate your market risk. Can the stock's value fall? (Yes.) How far? How much can I afford to lose? Should I set a goal for myself to cut losses if and when it does fall? The best way to manage risk is to set a bail-out position for yourself in case market risk does go against you.

2. *Liquidity risk.* This kind of risk comes in two types. Portfolio liquidity risk means you don't have enough capital free to take advantage of emerging opportunities. For example, whenever you are fully invested you simply cannot take advantage of any new opportunities unless you sell an existing position. There is nothing wrong with being fully invested, but this can create a liquidity challenge if you're unable to sell your existing positions at attractive prices to raise capital for new investments.

3. *Cash flow risk.* This refers to the problem of money management. For example, if you overinvest in high-risk positions using your margin

account, you might not have the money available to meet a margin call. This problem arises when you use too much borrowing to expand your open positions, becoming unable to keep up with the demands of interest payments and margin requirements.

4. *Diversification risk.* Two versions of diversification risk have to be kept in mind. The first and most obvious is the problems that arise when you do not diversify enough. In the next chapter, I will demonstrate how underdiversification represents a big threat, and I will also show you an array of ways to successfully diversify your investments. The second problem is overdiversification, a situation where an investor has too many positions and the performance of any one stock has little contribution to the overall gains of the entire portfolio. An example would be a portfolio of 50 positions. If one position gains 100 percent, and all the others remain flat, than the overall gain will be a small 2 percent, meaning that the big gains of one winner have little impact on the overall portfolio. If your portfolio is so broad that it represents the overall market, you are only going to profit at the same rate as the market, at best, and in some cases, your fund will underperform even with massive levels of diversification. The ETF is an effective means for investing in an entire sector, metal, country, or other identification. But here again, your overall income is only going to equal the net average of all the ETF components, including the overperformers and the underperformers. Picking just the right level of diversification is not easy, but it is a skill every investor should try to develop.

5. *Economic risk.* Anyone who has been through a recession—and this definitely includes everyone born before 2010—understands that an economic downturn can create a crash in the stock market, bringing down the valuations of both good companies and bad. When credit markets are tight, housing values are falling, and unemployment is increasing, everyone is afraid. Investors pull money out of the market and sit on the sidelines. Small businesses, including emerging small-cap companies, cannot borrow money, and even if they could, they often hesitate to invest in expansion, fearing that the recession will get worse. The apprehension makes the point that a lot of recessionary problems are self-fulfilling, but they are very real problems in every case. Most recessions last less than two years, but they seem longer if you are unemployed, in foreclosure, or losing value in your retirement account.

6. *Knowledge and experience risk.* The importance of going through markets, both good and bad, and mixing in profits with losses makes you wiser, even when the learning curve is painful. It's like your first trip to Las Vegas or Atlantic City; you get your real experience through time

playing cards at the table. If you suffer a loss, whether in small-cap investing or blackjack, you never expect it to occur, but when it does, you are transformed from naïve beginner into experienced and seasoned investor.

7. *Tax and inflation risk.* A final form of risk is among the most severe, but it is often invisible. It is the double impact of income taxes and inflation. Taken separately, they may seem relatively benign. But together, they can be disastrous. Inflation, which can be thought of as either higher prices or the loss of purchasing power, diminishes the value of your portfolio. The two aspects are merely different versions of the same problem. For example, in 2008, you would need $7.27 to equal the purchase power of one dollar in 1960. (To check the loss of purchasing power over time, use the free online calculator at www.measuringworth.com/ppowerus.)

Taxes also take away from purchasing power. The tax is based on your effective tax, which is all of your income minus adjustments, the standard or itemized deduction, and exemptions you are allowed. Taxable income is taxed anywhere from 10 percent up to 35 percent, not including state rates. If you are paying a relatively modest 15 percent federal rate and your state income tax is another 9 percent, you are paying 24 percent in taxes. Short-term gains are taxed at the individual's income tax rate, while long-term gains on investments held at least 12-months are taxed at a maximum rate of 15%. The tax code clearly encourages long-term investing, and when investing for big gains in small cap stocks, an investment outlook of greater than one-year is advisable for both the investment itself, and the tax benefits.

To appreciate the combined effect of inflation and taxes, calculate your breakeven rate of return. This is the rate you need to earn on your investments to break even after both inflation and taxes. The formula is

$$I \div (100 - R) = B$$
$$I = \text{ rate of inflation}$$
$$R = \text{ effective tax rate (federal and state)}$$
$$B = \text{ breakeven return}$$

For example, if you assume that average inflation based on the Consumer Price Index (CPI) is going to run at 3 percent in the future, and you pay federal and state taxes at the rate of 24 percent combined, your breakeven is 3.9 percent:

$$3\% \div (100 - 24) = 3.9\%$$

So a 1 percent certificate of deposit is going to lose money and keeping cash in your mattress also fails to keep up with inflation, even at very low rates. Remember, too, that this is the *average* return you need just to preserve your capital. So if you lose 5 percent on one-half of your portfolio, you need to earn 8.9 percent on the other half before you have any real profits.

The double effect of inflation and taxes is a serious matter, and many investors lose money without realizing it. The only solution is to find ways to beat the inflation and tax double effect, a reality that first led me to the potential in small caps.

Timing Decisions

You face two levels of decision-making in investing in small-cap stocks. First is the selection of candidates you believe offer the greatest value and growth potential. Second is the timing of buy and sell decisions. To a degree, making good use of limit and stop-loss orders helps protect you from extensive losses, but given the higher-than-average volatility of small caps, you need to be able to spot some of the timing trends that affect your overall profitability.

Tools That Improve Your Timing

Everyone needs tactical tools to improve their market timing. The combination of using the best protective orders, setting goals, and taking partial profits all help reduce possible losses.

Several ideas are useful in timing your buy and sell decisions. These include:

1. *Setting profit goals and bail-out points.* Any time you set a specific goal, you arm yourself with information about when and why you will buy and sell. You buy when trends you utilize meet a specific criteria: bargain price, profit point, or change in markets. You sell when you either reach a predetermined profit yield or when you lose down to a bail-out point.
2. *Decreasing level of holdings after a profitable run-up.* It often occurs that prices rise and you reach your goal, but the current financial indicators convince you that the trend is going to continue. You can cut potential losses by selling a portion of your holdings and letting the balance ride.

3. *Using trailing stop orders to control potential losses.* Losses can show up very suddenly, so you have to be diligent in watching fundamental and technical trends and looking for early signals of change. You further protect yourself by using trailing stops to set a floor on your potential losses.

4. *Reviewing and re-reviewing the fundamentals regularly.* You should never expect to draw a conclusion about a company and then never look at it again. This is especially true with small caps, where growth trends can be dramatic and fast. The fortunes of your small-cap portfolio can be meteoric in scope and speed, but they can go in the opposite direction just as quickly. So you need to enter into a program of regular review.

5. *Following financial trends and looking for leveling-out of those trends.* Every trend levels out at some point, and no trend is going to continue forever. Even in the best of situations, when profits bound ahead and stock prices follow, be vigilant in looking for subtle changes in the revenue, earnings, and other trends you monitor. You want to make your sell decisions *before* the change becomes obvious to everyone else, because by then the price decline has already occurred.

6. *Tracking moving averages and identifying buy and sell signals.* The use of moving averages is probably the strongest of the technical tools you can use. The averages offset short-term price volatility and show you what is likely to occur in the coming weeks or months. Changes in the moving averages can improve your timing of buy and sell decisions and should be watched closely.

In the last chapter, I provided you with a three-part timing strategy:

1. Three or more consecutive short-term trend periods.
2. Narrow range day.
3. Higher-than-average volume.

When these three conditions occur together, you have the strongest possible signal to trade on a technical basis. On the downtrend, these three signal a buy trade, and on the upside, they signal a sell.

Using Stock Options

The use of options is an increasingly popular strategy used by investors to not only protect their investments and generate income, but also to leverage their capital and generate outsized returns.

Stock options are a contract between a buyer and seller that provides a buyer with the right to buy or sell a stock at a later date, at a previously agreed upon price. In exchange for granting the option to the buyer, the seller is paid a premium by the buyer.

Investment decisions can be protected with the use of options for many purposes. First, you can protect paper profits by buying put options, which increase in value when the underlying stock's price falls, as a form of insurance; on the downside, you can take advantage of dips in price by buying calls, which increase in value when the value of the underlying stock rises. You can also go short on options, but this is a higher-risk strategy not appropriate for many traders because the options industry is very complex and risks are simply too high for most people.

Options are important tools to keep in mind for managing your portfolio and for mitigating market risk, even if you need to wait until today's small cap grows to the point that the options exchanges begin allowing traders to use options in addition to buying and selling shares. The volume of activity in options has grown tremendously in the past few years, and today options have become more mainstream than ever before. In fact, you can manage a small-cap portfolio by trading in options on sector ETF options or index options. This is indirect, but it does enable you to hedge risk on the broader market.

The second point to remember is that options are highly specialized. They contain a range of risks from high-risk to highly conservative, strategies are numerous, and the jargon of the options market is very specialized. Even knowing how to read an options quote and mastering the rules for avoiding unintended exercise of positions is complex. Before anyone gets into options trading, whether on individual stocks or on an ETF or index, they need to master the complexities of the market itself. One effective way to do this is to use one of many paper trading sites. The Chicago Board Options Exchange (CBOE, at www.cboe.com) offers a free paper trading service. Go to the CBOE site and click the link on "trading tools" and from there to the "paper money" page. By using this service, you can experience options trading in the real world, but without putting any of your money at risk. On the same site, you should download the free disclosure prospectus, *Characteristics and Risks of Standardized Options* (see the link at the bottom of the CBOE home page).

Timing is rarely going to be perfect. Beyond the use of protective orders and, possibly, options, you also need to accept the probability that some of your trades will be ill-timed. Everyone has bought too early or sold too soon (or too late), and only by recognizing the signs can you beat the odds. These signals include:

1. *Changes in the stock's trading range.* If you track the company's trading range, look for triangles showing either a broadening or narrowing range. These may foreshadow a breakout above or below current

trading levels. Another trading range trend worth note is any test of resistance or support. A breakthrough is a strong signal of an important change in price, especially if the price adjustment continues. An unsuccessful test indicates weakness and anticipates a move in the opposite direction. These easily spotted technical indicators are great aids to the timing of either buy or sell decisions.

2. *Significant or surprising earnings news.* Any time an earnings report is a surprise, it indicates that analysts were wrong or that management failed to forecast properly (or in some cases, withheld the news, usually the bad news). Do keep in mind that the smaller the market capitalization, the less likely it is that a company will have significant—or any—analyst coverage. This can make it trickier to identify a bona fide earnings surprise.

3. *Changes in management, markets, or competition.* These changes are usually quite important because they are going to affect the company's profitability and, consequently, the stock price. Any important change in these fundamentals should not be ignored.

4. *Unusual changes in daily volume.* Another technical indicator that can be very revealing is a sudden spike in volume. Increases in volume may be caused by new demand or by sudden and unexpected sell orders; it all depends on whether the stock price rises or falls with the unusual volume. The main point to remember is that volume spikes are always caused by something important, and they deserve closer attention and further investigation.

Trading Techniques

Timing is rarely perfect, even when you know the signs to look for and take action you think is right at the time. Because timing is not perfect, you can control your overall cost of buying stock by using averaging techniques. These should only be used for companies you believe have exceptional growth potential. An important concept to remember is that you do not want to invest more money in a company that is falling in value. If you have made a mistake, sell right away, learn from the mistake, and go on to the next company. But when your belief in a company remains strong, averaging can be a worthwhile strategy.

Dollar cost averaging is a technique in which the same dollar amount is invested in one company at regular intervals—monthly, for example. An analysis of the effect of this is that the average price is higher than current price, but it is always lower than original cost if the stock price declines, and creates a net basis below current value when the price rises.

For example, you buy $1,000 of stock in six consecutive months. During that time, the price trends downward:

Month	Investment Amount	Purchase Price	Average Price
1	$1,000.00	$14.15	$14.15
2	1,000.00	13.92	14.03
3	1,000.00	13.75	13.94
4	1,000.00	13.79	13.90
5	1,000.00	13.58	13.84
6	1,000.00	13.33	13.75

Note that dollar cost averaging in this example creates an average price per share that is always higher than the current market value. At this point, if you were to sell all 600 shares, you would make a small profit of 0.42, or $252 (0.42 × 600). In comparison, if you had bought 600 shares at the original price of $14.15, selling today would create a net loss of 0.82 per share (14.15 − 13.33) or $492.00 (0.82 × 600).

Dollar cost averaging when the stock's price is moving upward creates the opposite effect. The average price is always lower than the current market value. For example, given the same facts as above but in a rising market:

Month	Investment Amount	Purchase Price	Average Price
1	$1,000.00	$14.15	$14.15
2	1,000.00	14.22	14.19
3	1,000.00	14.53	14.30
4	1,000.00	14.67	14.39
5	1,000.00	14.90	14.49
6	1,000.00	15.26	14.62

The advantage here is that your average cost per share is $14.62. This is higher than it would have been if you had purchased 600 shares in the first month, but the system is designed to protect against price decline, while also averaging out the cost if prices move up. Here your average cost is $14.62 per share, but current price per share is $15.26, a paper profit of 0.64 per share, or $384 (0.64 × 600).

A similar technique is called value cost averaging. In this variation, the dollar value of monthly share purchase is adjusted based on how the stock performs. When the price declines, you buy more shares, and when it increases you buy fewer. This creates the overall effect of an average basis below current share price. It also improves your average rate of return when the price does increase well above your average.

With averaging techniques for stocks you have qualified as good value candidates, you can worry less about timing and more about growing profits for the long-term. Timing is an important issue because naturally you want to buy low and sell high. But if you are looking to the long-term and plan to hold your small caps as both growth and value portions of your portfolio, short-term timing is not as crucial an issue as the more critical stock selection itself.

You have a lot to think about as an investor. You have to master an array of different kinds of orders and decide which work best for you; identify many kinds of risk and determine your own risk tolerance. Most of all, you have to time your buy and sell decisions to make the best use of capital, avoid loss, and maximize your profits. All of these challenges rely on experience and selecting the best sources for information and insight.

The Bottom Line

- Small caps are illiquid, meaning there are fewer buyers and sellers than with larger stocks.
- Lower liquidity means more volatile fluctuations in price, which requires unique trading methods including the use of limit orders.
- Volatility can scare away many investors from small caps, but the long-term outperformance of small caps offsets the short-term volatility.
- Risk tolerance must be considered when evaluating small caps as a component of an investment portfolio.
- Timing is everything with investing—great investments are executed to maximize profit potential.

CHAPTER 8

Portfolio Diversification and Allocation

"The financial markets generally are unpredictable. So that one has to have different scenarios. The idea that you can actually predict what's going to happen contradicts my way of looking at the market."

—George Soros

"Wide diversification is only required when investors do not understand what they are doing."

—Warren Buffett

Small caps are my favorite among equity choices for reasons I have explained in this book. While I continue to hold to this belief, I do not put all of my eggs in one basket, since the risk would be overwhelming. It makes much more sense to diversify on several levels: by company and sector, company size, and investment type. Consider diversification not as a singular strategic action, but as a series of steps you take to spread risk and to reduce exposure by any sensible means.

Small caps properly belong in the portfolio of every investor interested in better-than-average growth. The decision to include or exclude any class of stocks is always appropriately based on risk tolerance, which evolves and changes over time. As a general rule, if you have a long time horizon for your investments, you will probably conclude that you should have more small caps in your portfolio than someone who expects to need access to their funds in the near future.

Diversification comes in many shapes and sizes, and as a smart investor you need to be aware of these variations. You need to achieve what I term *effective* diversification, which means that you not only spread money around among different stocks, but that you also make sure you are *actually* diversified. Effective diversification means that in any kind of market, a portion of your investments will be affected, but not all of your investments.

In this chapter I expand on the concept of diversification to also explain asset allocation, the division of investment capital among different markets and types of investments. Some financial advisers believe that the same asset allocation should apply to all investors, and they publish fixed percentages you should use in your portfolio given present market conditions. I believe differently. No two people have the same risk profile. Any assignment among equity, debt, real estate, and money markets is random because no one formula applies to everyone. I also like to make a fine distinction in the equity portion of the model, setting aside small caps as a portion of the equity component of an investment portfolio.

Financial advisers often recommend a classically balanced portfolio, which would be invested 60 percent in equities and 40 percent in fixed income. The equity component includes stocks, whether individual stocks, mutual funds, or electronically traded funds (ETFs). The fixed income component includes corporate bonds, municipal bonds, and treasuries, which can be purchased individually or through mutual funds or ETFs.

Equity Diversification Methods

You can diversify your portfolio in several ways, and may want to consider any of these as part of an extended diversification program. These methods include:

1. *Company-based.* Basic diversification is also the best known: buying shares in more than one company. A popular belief is that the more stocks in the portfolio, the lower the risk. But this isn't always true. If the broad market is subject to a sharp decline, then nearly all stocks are going to suffer. Look to 2008 as an example: Dozens of safe companies lost more than half their value in only a few months. When the market turns bearish, most equities decline, regardless of quality.

2. *By sector.* Many investors recognize that sectors do not all perform in the same manner or respond to economic or even market conditions identically. So for many who have observed this, diversifying by sector is an effective means for overcoming a general market bear trend. The dot com bust in 2000 affected mainly technology and Internet stocks, and many investors who invested primarily in these types of stocks suffered tremendous losses as a result.

3. *Economic, market, and political conditions or trends.* Yet another method is to pick stocks that react to different market trends in their own way. For example, a public utility company is going to be sensitive to interest rate trends; a retail chain is affected by unemployment and inflation; and defense contractors will have good or bad times based on the current sentiment in Washington concerning defense spending. Different political sentiments and levels of world unrest all affect

companies in varying degrees, so diversifying in a way to spread this risk makes sense.

4. *Mixing direct ownership with funds.* Buying mutual funds is widely practiced and has been popular for decades. Using mutual funds or ETFs, you essentially get diversified by owning multiple companies. If you own shares of mutual funds, ETFs, or variable annuities directly or through your retirement plan, you are not alone; millions of people use this as one of many ways to diversify. Using the same philosophy that favors small caps over large caps, you might consider using smaller, more aggressive funds. These will be more likely to beat the market, especially if the fund is operated by management with a track record of success.

5. *By attribute or location.* A subtle alternative is to diversify by choosing stocks with a specific attribute (management or speed of growth, for example) or by location (by country or region). This spreads risk in many additional ways and performs the same benefit that an ETF or mutual fund intends to perform, but with more control and without having to pay fees. Emerging markets have been increasingly popular places to invest, as investors seek opportunities providing greater growth. The BRIC countries (Brazil, Russia, India, and China) in particular have seen economic growth rates that far surpass that of the Western world.

6. *Based on capitalization.* Small caps tend to increase in value faster than other classes of stocks when coming out of a recession or bear market, and they provide a competitive mix in many other ways as well. For example, by definition, small caps are likely to have greater cash flow challenges than better capitalized competitors. Small-cap companies diversify your portfolio in terms of profit potential, cash flow, price strength, and both value and growth investment strategies.

Diversification Mistakes

Diversification is easier said than done. The concept is sensible and easy to comprehend, but more difficult to execute and maintain. Even when a portfolio is diversified effectively, over time that risk-reduction feature can evaporate as stocks are sold and replaced. Investors can easily forget to maintain diversification if only to reduce risk. Unfortunately, several factors get in the way. These include:

1. *Failure to manage.* The most common reason that diversification fails is the simple failure to manage. Diversification is never permanent. Any time a stock rises or falls in value, or when you buy or sell shares, the portfolio mix changes. For example, if you are diversified among three sectors and you sell one of the three, what do you do with the cash? If you buy shares of another company in one of the remaining sectors, the

mix is changed. Risks are increased, and in the event of a big market move you might discover that you were not monitoring your portfolio effectively enough. Status changes over time, so you need to keep an eye not only on today's situation, but also on emerging changes.

2. *The greed factor.* When a particular stock is rising in value (or when the whole market is moving upward) the temptation is to dump diversification and race to where the action is (or seems to be) to get all of the profits you can. Many investors and traders have fallen into the trap of putting all of their capital into a single stock or group of stocks that just "can't lose," but they can and do. Many investors made this fatal error during the tech stock boom of the 1990s and the real estate and financial bubble in the past decade.

3. *Unawareness of risk.* Before the meltdown of 2008, it surprised me that so many investors were unaware of the level of market risk they faced or of how to mitigate that risk. Some had the point of view that simply spreading money around among several different stocks was adequate, but it was not and is not. Risk itself is omnipresent in all kinds of markets, even very bullish ones (although many ignore risk in the euphoria of rising markets). You need to know how to effectively diversify with risk in mind and to treat diversification as a portfolio management tool and not just as a profit-creation device.

4. *Ineffective levels of diversification.* Even if you place capital in many different stocks and sectors, it does not necessarily mean you will achieve the risk mitigation you seek. If all of the sectors you pick are subject to the same kinds of economic and market risks, what is the point? True diversification is defined as investing money so that no one factor affects your entire portfolio in the same way. If this is not a feature of your portfolio, then you have not yet achieved diversification.

It is not enough to just own more than one stock in your portfolio. Some methods of diversification do not really protect against market cycles or outside economic events. For example, owning shares in three oil exploration companies is not effective diversification. All three are in the same industry. And neither is it effective diversification to own all small caps spread out among five sectors, without any exposure to other types of equities or fixed income.

Overdiversification

So if some diversification is good, a lot of diversification is better, right? In a word, no. A problem that many investors overlook is the threat of overdiversification. Most emphasis is placed on the lack of risk-spreading, but you can also diversify so much that your portfolio is likely to simply deliver average or below average returns.

Less Is More

More is not better when it comes to diversification. You can go too far, spreading capital around so widely that you end up with a return approximating the entire market. If your goal is to *beat* the market, diversifying too much contradicts that goal.

You can overdiversify in several ways. How many different stocks should you own? Is it better to invest $10,000 in five stocks or invest $1,000 in fifty stocks? Should you invest in one of the largest mutual funds you can find with billions of dollars under management, invested in hundreds of companies?

Having too many stocks or owning a mutual fund with a large number of holdings are examples of overdiversification. No matter what kind of market performance you experience in these cases, the good results are going to be offset by the bad. Consequently, your portfolio can rarely excel or beat the market. Overdiversification ensures that some of your holdings are going to underperform the average. Owning 50 stocks is a management chore, and it also destroys the intended purpose of diversifying. An extremely large mutual fund cannot sell enough shares quickly to avoid a price decline even when fund managers recognize problems. And the funds have to buy a large number of stocks because they have such a large cash base available but cannot take a controlling position in any one company. Most mutual funds are also very unlikely to ever have small-cap holdings of any merit for the same reasons. Although there are some outstanding mutual funds that are focused on small-cap stocks, have limited the size of their funds, and consistently delivery strong performance for their shareholders.

To avoid overdiversification, take a realistic view of risk itself. Market risk is going to be a factor no matter what you do, and diversification does not take this risk away. It reduces it, but if you go too far you will never beat the odds, either. Realistically, you know that you have to expose yourself to risk. But smart stock selection and reasonable levels of diversification ensure that risk is taken in an informed manner, and that you are more likely to benefit from a company's good management and rising stock prices.

Using Mutual Funds and ETFs to Diversify

Investing in mutual funds has always been viewed as an easy way to diversify. This is true in the sense that funds carry a portfolio of stocks selected by a fund manager who is thought to be an expert who is qualified to manage your investments.

The question of which fund to pick is a complex one. It relies on several important differences among the funds, including:

1. *Management's track record.* Effective managers earn their fees by out-performing the market in both good and bad times, therefore attracting more investors to their funds. Picking a fund that is run by competent managers is a sound method for narrowing the field. This provides diversification, but it also attempts to ensure that you get your money's worth with good performance. The whole idea behind funds is that management is supposed to do a good job; so always seek exceptional performance as a way to make your selection.

2. *The portfolio and stated fund objectives.* Funds are classified in many ways: growth, income, value, aggressive, conservative, large-cap, small-cap, country or region. Be sure the fund you pick matches your objectives in terms of risk profile and also focuses on the kinds of stocks and bonds that you need and want in your portfolio. Picking the right fund helps you meet your objectives while accomplishing effective diversification.

3. *The size of the portfolio.* Many funds are mega-sized, which may reflect good marketing, or past successes in making money for their shareholders, and therefore attracting new investors. When it comes to investing in small-cap funds, the smaller funds often have an advantage. As small-cap funds outperform, more investors are attracted based upon the track record and invest with the manager. As the fund expands and manages more capital, it becomes harder to find enough attractive investments that meet the goals of the fund. Because small caps are by definition small in size, a fund can be limited in terms of the size of its investment. For this reason, many small-cap funds perform best in their early years, and as their asset base grows due to their success, the performance declines. For this reason, some small-cap funds close their doors to new investors once a certain level of capital has been reached. You are probably better off staying with very small funds and even closed-end funds (those that do not accept any new shares after a specified portfolio size has been reached) that otherwise meet your investment criteria.

4. *Types of investments.* Compare the stated objective of a fund detailed in its prospectus to your own investing goals to make sure it's a good match for you. Objectives like "conservative growth" or "income" have specific meaning, and you need to ensure that these are in line with what you need and want.

5. *The various fees and charges that apply.* This is where fund selection gets tricky. The biggest of all fees—the sales load—should be avoided

without question. You can pick your own mutual fund without having to pay an 8.25 percent fee right off the top; there are plenty of no-load funds that have performed just as well as load funds. There are additional fees to be concerned with, fees that come in a vast array and often are not at all clear in what they mean. You need to be able to make an apples-to-apples comparison. I suggest you use a calculator to compare the real cost of different funds. One excellent free calculator is offered by the SEC and can be accessed online at www.sec.gov/investor/tools/mfcc/mfcc-int.htm.

The fees that management charges for its services vary greatly, and anyone buying fund shares needs to make comparisons of all fees, including load, 12b.1 fees, expenses, and special charges. Most load funds take the sales commission right off the top, meaning less of your money goes into the investment. Others charge a deferred sales load. If you sell shares within a specified number of years, the back-end load is deducted from your proceeds. Normally, if you hold shares beyond the specified date, the load is not applied.

You also can limit your selection by picking mutual funds that have been top performers in recent years. Yahoo provides a summary of the best performing small-cap funds. The following tables summarize these as of the beginning of 2009. For more updated lists, go to http://biz.yahoo.com/p/top.html:

Small-Cap Growth Funds, Top Performers 5 Years:
- Royce 100 Svc (RYOHX)
- Fidelity Advisor Small Cap I (FSCIX)
- Wells Fargo Advantage Small Cap Opp Adm (NVSOX)
- Schroder U.S. Opportunities Inv (SCUIX)
- Van Kampen Small Cap Growth A (VASCX)
- Fidelity Advisor Small Cap A (FSCDX)
- Fidelity Advisor Small Cap T (FSCTX)
- Van Kampen Small Cap Growth B (VBSCX)
- Van Kampen Small Cap Growth C (VCSCX)
- Fidelity Advisor Small Cap C (FSCEX)

Small-Cap Value, Top Returns, Five Years:*
- Pinnacle Value (PVFIX)
- Paradigm Value (PVFAX)
- Allianz NFJ Small Cap Value Instl (PSVIX)

*Source: http://biz.yahoo.com

- Allianz NFJ Small Cap Value Admin (PVADX)
- Allianz NFJ Small Cap Value A (PCVAX)
- Allianz NFJ Small Cap Value D (PNVDX)
- GAMCO Westwood Mighty Mites AAA (WEMMX)
- Allianz NFJ Small Cap Value R (PNVRX)
- GAMCO Westwood Mighty Mites A (WMMAX)
- Allianz NFJ Small Cap Value B (PCVBX)

The ETF is a relatively new kind of investment. Traditional mutual funds set their level of portfolio investment and diversification based on decisions made by management (and paid for by shareholders). Shares are bought and sold directly between investors and fund managers based on the close-of-day net asset value (NAV) of the fund. Mutual funds require a lot of research, analysis, and trading expertise, and therefore the costs associated with these investments tend to be high.

An ETF on the other hand preidentifies the target portfolio holdings, which often includes a basket of stocks, bonds or a commodities, which do not change unless there is a merger or acquisition, or a component drops out of the list. Once the ETF is set up, there isn't much in the form of ongoing research or analysis, since the investments are predefined. Shares are bought and sold on public stock exchanges, making ETF trading quite flexible. ETFs are often used to trade stock or bond indices, commodities, or sectors of the market. Many also offer options trading. Unlike mutual funds that are priced at the end of the trading session, ETFs trade throughout the day in the same manner as stocks, making them a more attractive option than mutual funds for active traders. Additionally, fees for ETFs are lower due to limited management and research.

A Convenient Way of Investing

The ETF makes mutual fund investing convenient and more predictable, with its preidentified basket of stocks. Even beyond stocks, you can use ETFs to diversify among indices, commodities, and whole market sectors.

There are dozens of specialized ETFs available, including commodities such as gold, silver, and oil, emerging stock markets such as China and India, stock market indices such as the S&P 500 and the Wilshire 5000, and stocks within sectors such as gold miners or technology stocks.

Small-cap ETFs that you should be aware of are:

- iShares Russell 2000 Index (IWM)
- iShares Russell Microcap Index (IWC)
- iShares S&P SmallCap 600 Index (IJR)
- SPA Market Grader Small-Cap 100 (SSK)
- First Trust Small Cap Core AlphaDEX (FYX)
- PowerShares Dynamic Small Cap (PJM)
- RevenueShares Small Cap (RWJ)

Risk Tolerance as a Means for Diversifying Your Portfolio

When you think about diversification, you probably limit your analysis to products—stocks, bonds, money market, mutual funds, ETFs—and to industries or other subgroups. But also consider the possibility of diversification by risk tolerance.

Most people describe their investing style or holdings as conservative, moderate, or aggressive. But it is rarely a simple matter of wanting *all* of your investments to fit a single category. Investors aim to achieve a desired risk profile based on their objectives. And the risk profile can be achieved by using various investment tools including stocks, bonds, mutual funds, and ETFs. For example, even a conservative investor might include a small portion of their investments for growth or emerging markets stocks, even though these are considered to be more risky.

For investors seeking to outperform the market as a whole, they must be more aggressive, growth oriented, or contrarian in a portion of their portfolio. While that portion may be a small piece of the total portfolio, it is required for investors who aim to beat the market. They might want to take exceptional risks by purchasing shares of very volatile stocks, playing the options market, or buying commodity futures. Some others, leaning more to the conservative side of the spectrum, will prefer putting the balance into certificates of deposit or Treasury securities or in shares of well-established blue chip companies paying high dividends.

The point to keep in mind is that diversification is rarely a solid, consistent practice. This is because risk itself cannot be easily defined in a way that an entire portfolio will match a specific risk level. This lack of diversification may be just as dangerous as putting all of your capital into a single stock. Given the reality that the stock market inevitably goes through periods of high volatility, varying the risk level within the market simply makes sense. This augments my previous observation that small-cap companies can serve a purpose in most portfolios; it is only the percentage of small-cap holding that is going to vary.

If you have all of your investment capital concentrated in only a couple sectors, your risk exposure is intense. And consider what happens when the market, as a whole, is on the decline. During bear markets when the stock market crashes, prices of all stocks often fall. And in a recession such as the one experienced in 2008 and 2009, not only did stocks plunge, but so did bonds, commodities, and real estate. There was truly no place to hide, as the value of all assets came crashing down. Even a diversified portfolio can get crushed in the worst of times, demonstrating that diversification isn't a fool proof solution to limiting losses.

Diversification by risk tolerance—is a surprising idea to many people. But think for a moment about what risk really means. It is the exposure to danger in some form. So in the market, are you content to having all of your capital exposed to the same market risk? Doesn't it make more sense to diversify by different assumptions about risk? You may vary holdings between shares of small caps and other kinds of stock (assuming markets are likely to rise over time) and precious metals like gold (buying shares of SPDR Gold Shares – GLD, for example) on the assumption that a weakening dollar will mean greater value in gold. You would find it unacceptable to invest all of your money in gold, so by the same argument, why are you willing to invest all of your money in stocks?

Asset Allocation Basics

Asset allocation, an expanded concept gaining popularity in recent years, is a form of diversification in which you divide your overall investment portfolio among completely different types of securities to achieve a desired investment return and risk profile. The most common of these are equities (stocks), fixed income (bonds and Treasury securities), money market, cash, and real estate. This is an important concept because, as the stock market has taught everyone, it is not always wise to put all of your eggs in one basket. All markets are cyclical, and all respond to different events. For example, when you consider the history of strength or weakness among stocks, bonds, real estate, and the money market (the four usual classes of allocation), it is clear that they can operate independently of one another.

Three points should be emphasized about asset allocation:

1. *The concept should be determined individually and not applied universally.* Asset allocation as a means for distributing capital among different investment products should be a highly personalized procedure. So when I see the advice to have "50 percent equities, 40 percent fixed income, 5 percent real estate, and 5 percent cash," it makes me wonder: Why should this apply to everyone? In fact, asset allocation works within the definitions of your risk profile and your individual assumptions about the market at a given point in time.

2. *Real estate should be included in the mix.* You probably have the majority of your available capital tied up in your own home, or plan to at some point in the future. This means a major allocation of your capital is going to go to real estate. Historically, this has been a great idea because real estate (at least before 2008) beat most other markets, and once the recessionary trend has ended, real estate is likely to stabilize. You can take another approach by leaving your personal home out of the allocation mix and then assigning portions of your capital to real estate through real estate investment trusts (REITs) or real estate ETFs.
3. *Stocks are considered a singular category.* The biggest problem for me with asset allocation is the treatment of equities as a single market. I think it makes more sense to allocate among a number of different kinds of stock investments. These include small-cap direct ownership, mid-cap and/or large-cap companies, and mutual funds or ETFs as separate categories. Within those categories, you also need to define whether you want to use a fund or ETF. Only by dividing up the equity portion into relevant but separate classes can you truly diversify your portfolio.

The benefit of allocation, as an expanded and long-term view of portfolio diversification, is that it helps you to view your investments in terms of the larger economy and not solely as a means for finding immediate profits. As a small-cap investor, you can make the best use of this idea by determining how to allocate your equity portfolio between small cap and other categories of stocks (large-cap, mid-cap, or mutual funds, for example).

Diversification and allocation are important tools for portfolio management. The purpose of these devices is risk mitigation. It is important, of course, to reduce overall risk by spreading it among different portions of the broader market and, as I mentioned earlier, to even diversify by levels of risk itself. The exercise of diversification will improve your portfolio's overall performance and help you to avoid catastrophic losses when markets do turn unexpectedly.

The Bottom Line

- Small caps must be included in every growth-oriented portfolio.
- Portfolio diversification is important for investors of all demographics.
- Age, time to retirement, risk tolerance, and financial goals must be considered when making portfolio allocation decisions.
- The small-cap component of a portfolio can achieve diversification using individual stocks, mutual funds, and ETFs.
- Small-cap mutual funds provide access to numerous small-cap stocks, hand selected by fund managers who charge a fee to managing the portfolio.
- Small-cap ETFs provide similar diversification at a lower fee, using baskets of predefined stocks.

CHAPTER 9

Buy Small Caps to Grow Your Portfolio

"Any man who is a bear on the future of this country will go broke."
—J.P. Morgan

"If a business does well, the stock eventually follows."
—Warren Buffett

The end goal of every investor is nearly always identical: to make profitable investments. Whether buying large caps or small caps, day trading or buy and hold investing, growth or value investing, it is all a means to generating profits by making smart investment decisions.

Investors are in a way competing against one another, buying a security today with the intention of selling it to someone else at some time in the future at a higher price. Your success is predicated upon your ability to have others place a higher value on your assets in the future.

The information world is flat. Investors around the world have equal access to publicly available news, financial, and performance metrics from companies. The Internet and Sarbanes-Oxley legislation leveled the playing field for equal access to information, meaning that the individual investor in Duluth, Minnesota, is able to obtain the same news and data about a stock as a hedge fund manager in New York with $10 billion under management. It is no longer access to information that gives you an edge over another investor; it is your ability to find the right information about the right companies, while filtering out the 99.9 percent that is irrelevant.

When it comes to finding and evaluating information that may give you a leg up on the big institutional investors, it is unlikely that it will be with well-known companies like Google, Microsoft, Wal-Mart, or Starbucks. These large caps have numerous analysts, financial journalists, and institutional investors watching their every move. Why? Because these are the largest, most widely owned stocks, and the big investors definitely own a piece.

It is the small, unknown companies that provide you with an edge, because by the nature of their size they are ignored by the vast majority of investors, even if their financial results are impressive.

Looking back at some of my best performing small-cap winners, these companies all had the signs of success: growing revenues, expanding profit margins, cash flow from operating activities, and downright inexpensive valuations. Yet these companies continued to fly under the radar of most investors for months, if not years, before being recognized as great stocks, whose share prices subsequently rose rapidly.

A Track Record of Small-Cap Success

I want to share with you a few of my best performing small-cap investments, so you can see that the system I've shared with you can truly produce outstanding gains that you are unlikely to find in mid- and large-cap stocks.

Ticker	Company Name	Return
TRLG	True Religion	2,218%
JCOM	j2 Global Communications	746%
RATE	Bankrate.com	705%
PEY-UN	Peyto Energy	649%
LEXR	Lexar Media	444%
GSB	Globalscape	376%
FRG	Fronteer Development	314%
FWHT	FindWhat	311%
IIG	iMergent	251%
NUAN	Nuance Communications	276%

I was able to achieve these remarkable gains using my simple eight-step system for finding great small-cap investments. I've shared this easy-to-use system with you through this book, and I hope you'll use this as you seek out small caps with big potential for growth and profits.

Step 1: *Growth Trends:* Identify growth trends and market sectors positioned for rapid growth in the years to come.

Step 2: *Finding Potential Winners:* Screen more than 7,000 publicly traded companies to find those companies that are unknown performers and are positioned to grow.

Step 3: *Fundamentals Matter:* Understand the fundamentals of the potential investment, including products, services, and management's ability to run the business.

Step 4: *Financial Performance:* Review and evaluate key metrics in a company's financial statements to understand historical financial performance.

Step 5: *Earnings Quality:* Look for red flags that indicate financial manipulation or fraud to avoid investing in a small-cap lemon.

Step 6: *Growth Outlook:* Develop an understanding of expectations for growth to make valid valuation comparisons.

Step 7: *Technical Analysis:* Understand the technical indicators of share price movements helps timing of investments and maximizes profits while limiting losses.

Step 8: *Pulling the Trigger:* Determine the optimal timing for entering new positions by using effective trading strategies.

Every investor focused on portfolio growth and capital appreciation must consider small caps as an opportunity. The reason is that these smaller companies are the driving force of growth in the U.S. economy, creating jobs, developing new products, and solving the market's problems.

In part due to their size, small companies are often capable of faster rates of growth than larger companies. It is the rapid growth that tends to propel shares of small-cap stocks higher, and creates the big profit opportunities for anyone invested before the positive news of financial results become widely known and the share price moves higher.

The Key Drivers to Growth

Growth in revenues and earnings are the key drivers of stock prices over the long term. Valuation metrics such as price-to-sales and price-to-earnings or discounted cash flow multiples may rise or fall over time with market sentiment. But there remains one consistent truth: Companies that grow their revenues and earnings over the long-term will see shares of their stock appreciate considerably.

No matter what indicators you use to find good values, it invariably comes down to revenues and earnings. These key drivers of a stock's price over the long-term directly affect share prices. This is a simple and powerful truth about investing.

If you look at the biggest stock market successes of all time—companies like Cisco, Dell, Microsoft, and Wal-Mart—not only have their shares risen impressively since the time of their IPOs, but their revenues and earnings have similarly increased at an incredible pace. The long-term rise in stock price is highly correlated with the increase in financial results.

This remains true for most top-performing investments over the long-term, not just the very best performing stocks. Two of my top-performing stock picks that I presented to my subscribers, and have discussed at length in this book, are BankRate (Nasdaq: RATE) and True Religion Apparel (Nasdaq: TRLG). You'll notice that the correlation between a rise in revenue and earnings is intact, as shown by the increase in both.

BankRate shares rose 5,500 percent from July 2002, when I presented the company to my subscribers, reaching a high of $55 in 2008. During this time, revenues increased 1,012 percent from $15 million in 2001 to $166.9 million in 2008, while EPS increased from -$0.07 to $1.01.

Meanwhile, shares of True Religion Apparel rose 3,100 percent from August 2004, when I presented the company to my subscribers, reaching a high of $31 in 2008. During this time, revenues increased 875 percent from $27.7 million in 2004 to $270 million in 2007, while EPS increased 815 percent from $0.20 to $1.83

Note that the share price of these companies rose at a faster rate than the underlying rate of growth for revenues and earnings. The reason is simple: Valuation multiples increased as the companies became larger with a proven track record of success.

Many investors, individual and institutional alike, tend to follow the herd, buying what others are buying, in sectors that are in favor, and stocks that are performing well. As they begin buying these performing stocks, small caps with great stories and a couple years of strong financial performance, the share price increases and valuation multiples jump. This means that instead of a stock trading at 20-times EPS, the valuation multiple may increase to 25 or 30-times EPS or in some cases, much higher.

Multiple expansion is one of the best ways to capture quick profits. As a company becomes well known, and is shown to be a proven winner, more investors flock to the stock. And when there are more buyers than sellers, prices rise. It is a simple case of supply and demand. This is so often the case with great small caps that become discovered by institutional investors, or even individual investors who read about them in widely read publications.

At first glance, a follow-the-herd approach can appear safe; after all, doing the same as everyone means you're doing the right thing. Right? Wrong. This strategy doesn't lead to outsized profits. It leads to mediocre performance as a result of purchasing good companies at outlandish valuations. Once investors have piled into a stock, declaring it a surefire winner, the valuation has often increased to the point where even the slightest hint of bad news can send investors to the sidelines, and rein in valuation multiples resulting in a collapsing share price.

Early Bird Gets the Worm

The best approach to making big profits is to get in on great growth stocks during the early stage—perhaps after only one or two quarters of solid financial outperformance. Fundamental research and due diligence provide you with the wherewithal to determine if this performance was a fluke or the beginning of a long-term growth trend. If it is the latter, then it is time to jump in and start buying if the fundamentals are strong and valuation is attractive. Investors who wait for many quarters or years of proven performance end up overpaying for these same stocks down the road. Warren Buffett wrote so eloquently, "If you wait for the robins, spring will be over." This is certainly applicable to small caps.

The winning strategy of the successful small-cap investor is to place bets on the unknown gems that are poised to become tomorrow's winners. The hints are available for investors to find, you just need to look for them all of the time and in the right places.

Not every small cap that appears poised for success will turn into a winner. There are many factors contributing to a successful stock, and conversely, many that can negatively impact the performance of a company. These include the global economy, industry or sector pressures, currency or commodity exposure, mismanagement, distribution challenges, and an ineffective marketing plan. No matter how in-depth your due diligence, it is not possible to know everything. And even if you do know everything, it is impossible to predict future performance. As investors, it is our job to develop a thesis for the future and to find opportunities with the greatest chance of success.

For this reason, portfolio diversification must be a part of every investor's strategy for successful investing. And within the small-cap portion of an overall portfolio, diversification is important. If you only own one small-cap stock, and have bet your entire small-cap portfolio allocation on that stock, you face significant risk. If the stock proves to be a winner, it will have an incredibly positive affect on the portfolio as a whole. But on the flip side, if the stock under-performs, it will drag down an otherwise fine portfolio.

Diversification in small caps can be accomplished in three different ways:

1. Own 5–15 individual small-cap stocks.
2. Own one or more small-cap mutual funds, which typically own 50–200 individual stocks.
3. Own small-cap ETFs, such as the iShares Russell 2000, which includes 2,000 individual small-cap stocks.

Of course, a combination of these three can also be employed, for example, by owning three individual stocks, a small-cap mutual fund, and an ETF.

Too much diversification can limit the performance of any single position, and for this reason I typically aim to have no more than 10 individual small caps in my personal portfolio—many more than this is just too many stocks to follow, and the profits from the winners will be diluted among the losers.

History proves that small caps outperform all other classes of equities over the long-term. While short-term volatility may be greater with individual small caps, a diversified portfolio of small-cap stocks will outperform over time, demonstrating that these are in fact relatively less risky investments than mid- or large-cap stocks.

The recession of 2008 and 2009 sent all stocks lower, and small caps led the way down. In 2008, the Russell 2000 Index, the barometer for small-cap stocks, fell 59 compared with losses of 53 for the Dow Jones Industrial Average, and 56 for the S&P 500.[1]

While the decline of small caps is often steeper going into a period of economic slowdown, the performance coming out of a downturn is much better, and small caps outperform. According to a T. Rowe Price report entitled *A Perspective On Financial Topics For Our Investors*, in the 12-month period following the end of the last nine recessions, small-cap stocks on average gained 24 percent, compared with a 17.6 percent gain for the S&P 500.[2]

And in another study from Merrill Lynch of the 18 bear markets since the 1930s, small caps posted an average gain of 41.4 percent in the 12 months after the end of the decline, compared with a median gain of 32.4 percent for large caps.

The good news is that after a poor showing in recent years, most investors are less interested in these small, unknown companies now then they were in the past. This further emphasizes the opportunity for you. Small caps led the markets lower in 2008, and if history proves any guide, they will lead the markets higher on the way out of the recession.

History Repeats Itself

History has shown that small caps lead markets out of recessions. This is a revealing fact, and it should point the way to future price appreciation as well. This is one of those instances where past performance might just serve as a good indicator of future movement.

Investors perceive small caps as being more risky in times of uncertainty, and thus have moved away from these toward safer investments, including larger blue chip equities and fixed income, such as U.S. Treasuries and corporate bonds. When the going gets tough, investors want comfort securities, well-known investments that are likely to fair well in good times and bad. During bear markets, capital preservation often becomes goal number one. Investors become more risk-averse, avoiding small, unknown companies with a great story and a couple of quarters of good financial performance. They instead want the proven winners, those known quantities that the stock market pundits mention on CNBC, Bloomberg, and Fox Business News.

Every investor needs small caps to recover from the losses in the stock market. The big gains in coming years will be generated by small, growth-oriented stocks trading at attractive values. Investors seeking growth in their portfolios simply must invest in this class of equities if they plan to recover from the recent market decline.

Like most investors, I've had my share of winners and losers. My goal is to limit the losses of my investments, while maximizing the upside by holding onto great companies for the longer term.

I know every investor could use a few stocks that provide triple-digit gains in their portfolios, in good times and bad. The only way to find stocks capable of big gains is in small-cap land, which is why if you focus your portfolio on growth, small caps must be included in the mix. Small caps are the solution, and history shows us that it is this class of equities that tends to recover first and rise the highest as the market turns around.

Opportunities are plentiful for astute investors in small-cap stocks. The big winners of the future are those companies that are currently small caps and have yet to rise to greatness. Your mission is to go out and find these great small caps before they are discovered by others. Using the tools that I've shared with you in *The Small-Cap Investor*, you are armed to discover these great companies of tomorrow and make intelligent decisions in your investment portfolio that will set you up for big gains in the coming years.

The Bottom Line

- Small caps outperform all other classes of equities over the long-term, making them an ideal investment for long-term investors.
- The big stock market winners of tomorrow are the small caps of today that will soar as their revenues and earnings expand.
- Financial performance, including revenue and earnings growth, is the single greatest factor contributing to the gains in individual stocks.
- Following a bear market, small caps emerge as the best performing class of equities.
- Investors seeking portfolio appreciation must own small caps because it is these companies that have the greatest prospects for outsized growth.

SmallCapInvestor.com PRO

20-Questions for Successful Investing

When evaluating a small-cap stock as an investment opportunity, it's important to ask yourself the tough questions before buying the stock. Use this list of questions as a tool when evaluating small caps for consideration in your investment portfolio.

...

---

1. Is the company operating in a high-growth sector? Do independent industry research estimates show a healthy growth trend?

2. How do you expect the company to perform compared with competitors?

3. Does the company sell a product with significant market potential? Is there enough demand to support continued expansion?

4. Is the company generating revenues? Are the revenues growing?

5. Are the costs increasing? Are they growing at a slower pace than revenues?

6. Is cash flow from operations positive? It is increasing?

7. Does the balance sheet show enough cash to allow growth without additional debt or equity offerings?

8. How does the financial performance compare with others in the industry?

9. Is management buying or selling the stock? Are they truly invested with shareholders?

10. Is executive compensation in-line with the financial performance of the company and its stock?

11. Are financial disclosures easy to understand? Is the company using off-balance sheet entities to hide the true financial performance?

12. Do analyst estimates or company guidance indicate continued growth in the next 12–24 months?

13. Does the company have a history of meeting or exceeding financial guidance?

14. Is management aggressive or conservative with their accounting? Do they push the limits of GAAP?

15. Does the stock chart indicate that now is the best time to buy? Or will patience results in a better entry price?

16. Is the stock hitting resistance or finding support at the current price? Is daily share volume increasing or decreasing?

17. Are there institutional investors who own the stock? Are they buying or selling the stock?

18. How does this small-cap stock fit into your overall investment portfolio and diversification strategy?

19. Are you prepared to own this stock for the long-term? Or are you trying to speculate for short-term profits?

20. If the stock market closed for the next five years, would you be happy owning this company?

Use this list of questions every time you're evaluating a small-cap stock. You can download this form in electronic format on my web site www.smallcapbook.com.

Notes

Chapter 1: Start Small, Finish Big—Discover Big Profits in Small-Cap Stocks

1. National Science Foundation, Division of Science Resources Statistics. 2008. "Research and Development in Industry: 2005," http://www.nsf.gov/statistics/industry.
2. "Tracking Stock Market Performance Through Past Economic Recessions," *T. Rowe Price Report*, Spring 2008.
3. http://www.safehaven.com/article-4524.htm.

Chapter 2: Big Ideas for Big Profits

1. Peter Townsend, *Further Up the Organization*, New York: Knopf, 1984.

Chapter 3: Finding Great Small-Cap Stocks

1. http://findarticles.com/p/articles/mi_m0EIN/is_2000_April_26/ai_61689930/.

Chapter 5: Financial Projections and Valuations

1. Ambrose Bierce, *The Devil's Dictionary*, New York: Doubleday, 1906.

Chapter 9: Buy Small Caps to Grow Your Portfolio

1. *T. Rowe Price Report*, Issue No. 99, Spring 2009, http://www.troweprice.com/gcFiles/pdf/04779-Spring08-final.pdf?scn=2008&rfpgid=7949&ft=GNL_CTT.
2. Ibid.

About the Author

I an Wyatt is an entrepreneur, investor, and small-cap investing expert. He is the founder of Business Financial Publishing, named #185 on the prestigious *Inc. Magazine* Inc. 500 list of the fastest-growing privately held companies in the United States in 2008. Ian is the editor and chief investment strategist of SmallCapInvestor.com. He lives in Vermont with his wife, Carrie. For more information, visit www.ianwyatt.com

Index